The Mississippi Gulf Coast and Neighboring Sites

Spots of Interest for Visitors and Locals

Twenty-five essays featuring landmarks, favorite tourist sites, and attractions on and near the Mississippi Coast.

A production of the Gulf Coast Writers Association

Editor: Philip L. Levin, MD

Publishing Info

The Mississippi Gulf Coast and Neighboring Sites

Published by Doctor's Dreams Publishing, P.O. Box 952, Long Beach, MS 39560, USA.

Manufactured in the United States of America

Graphic Layout and Formatting:
WONGA Studios, LLC - 1114 41st Avenue – Gulfport, MS 39501
http://www.WongaStudios.com

Printed by Pacom; South Korea: Pacifica Communications:
http://eng.gopacom.com

Cover Art: Photograph by Philip L. Levin, MD

ISBN: 978-0-9834396-8-4
LOC: 2013947698

Copies are available wholesale from our website:
http://www.GulfCoastAuthors.com

Or retail from Doctor's Dreams Publishing:
http://www.DoctorsDreams.net

Introduction

The Mississippi Coast provides its residents and visitors with an astonishing variety of culture, cuisine, and consideration. Its abundance of Southern charm and its deliberate pace compliment an immense variety of opportunities for visitors and locals to enjoy the history and joy of living in paradise. In the past ten years, we've suffered through the devastation of Hurricane Katrina, followed by an economic morass, and topped by an unfortunate oil spill, with our citizens shrugging them off to resume our determined comfortable way-of-life.

The Gulf Coast Writers Association, established in 1985, is the largest writers' association in the state. With this, our fifth annual anthology, we continue to promote local authors by providing opportunities to publish and tell of the home they love. This book sought input from hundreds of authors, with the simple guideline of writing about something you love on the Mississippi Gulf Coast. We're delighted at the diversity of the twenty-five chosen articles, and certain our readers will find them instructive and entertaining.

We are most grateful for the Deepwater Horizon Organization for providing the grant funding this book through our 501(c)(3) division, Gulf Coast Authors. A special thanks goes to our proofreaders, Grace B. Lebo and MyLien Nguyen, and our computer graphics specialist, Thomas Parker with WONGA Studios. For further information on Gulf Coast Writers, please check our website www.gcwriters.org, or contact us at gcwriters@aol.com and request a complimentary issue of our magazine, *The Magnolia Quarterly.*

Table of Contents

Pensacola Beach, Florida

Melissa Carrigee – Diamondhead, MS

Full of sun, sand, sea, great food and history, Pensacola Beach will wrap its white sugar-like sand around your feet and never let you go. Whether you are single, married, young or old, with kids or without, local or tourist, enjoy this city's offering of a wide variety of things to do and places to go. Or just pull up a hammock and enjoy the best of what Florida has to offer: sun and relaxation.

The first documented European visitor was Don Tristan de Luna in the summer of 1559, who brought with him eleven ships loaded with gear, food and settlers, though the colony was forced to abandon the site due to a hurricane. For the next four hundred years, Pensacola Beach developed slowly until 1931, when a recreation complex was built and named Pensacola Beach Casino, though simply called "The Casino." In 1972 the complex was demolished but the name "Casino Beach" still remains with the locals.

Pensacola Beach, Florida, has been ranked among the best beaches in the country by Trip Advisor (http://www.tripadvisor.com/TravelersChoice-Beaches). Pensacola Beach offers a wide variety of dining choices, as well as many choices in entertainment and activities, including fishing, sailing, paddle boarding, boogie boarding, windsurfing, parasailing, snorkeling, scuba diving, miniature golf, and go-karts.

Plenty of rental houses are available as well as condos and hotel rooms. Don't forget the good deals on renting a house or condo from an owner. You can check out listings at www.vrbo.com

The Margaritaville Beach Hotel is one of the newest hotels on the beachfront. You don't have to be a Jimmy Buffet fan to enjoy your stay at this island resort. Enjoy beautiful views of the Gulf of Mexico, great food in the hotel restaurant, and a laidback atmosphere that welcomes bathing suits and flip-flops. The choices are plenty for any type of visit you would like: a family vacation, a romantic getaway, a retreat, business trip, or a weekend getaway – the possibilities are endless.

Awaken to the magical sound of the ocean. The waves crash against the shore and seagulls chant "mine, mine, mine" as they fly through the air looking for their breakfast of crabs or fish, maybe even both. Crabs and fish for breakfast? Everything is possible at Pensacola Beach. Maybe you prefer waffles and pancakes (more suited for human tastes). Restaurants abound at the beach offering simple and refined waterfront dining at its best. Have a craving for a bucket of crab legs and local atmosphere? Ahoy Mateys, look no further than Peg Leg Pete's. One of Pensacola Beach's local hot spots, Peg Leg Pete's offers delicious food in a fun environment. Enjoy inside or outside dining, live music, a place for the kids to play, a bar, a store and the Lafitte Cove Marina. Yes, people come by boat, foot, or wheels to visit this local treasure. Visit their website to see all they have to offer, http://www.peglegpetes.com.

One can't visit Florida without going on a dolphin tour. Chase-N-Fin is an aquatic charter that cruises along the Gulf and Bay area as those aboard watch for dolphins. The wonderful and exciting experience of seeing dolphins swim and play around the boat usually lasts two to three hours. Advanced reservations are required. Please visit http://www.chase-n-fins.com for more information.

Next to dolphin watching, what would a beach trip be without a stroll on the popular Quietwater Beach Boardwalk? At the center of the boardwalk a giant shell serves as the background for the amphitheater, now an iconic Pensacola Beach landmark (perfect for pictures). Surrounding the amphitheater on both sides are restaurants, bars, clothing stores, souvenir stores, unique jewelry stores, art, gifts, surf wear and more. The boardwalk is located on the bay and is centrally located for easy access. Rent a bike and cruise along one of the world's largest barrier islands. Enjoy the sea air and numerous beach stores that line the main road.

Cruise around and find a favorite local hangout and enjoy the beach nightlife. With numerous places to go one will be able to find plenty of live music and cool drinks. Bamboo Willie's Beachside Bar is a local favorite. Fun during the day and night, Bamboo Willie's is located on the Quietwater Beach Boardwalk and offers live music, dancing, crawfish and original drinks (as well as your old favorites). Be sure to try the local favorite drink called the Bushwacker. Visit their website at http://www.bamboowillies.com.

Drive west on Fort Pickens Rd. (about ten miles) and you will arrive at historic Fort Pickens, which used to guard the entrance of Pensacola Bay. Built to defend the bay and its navy yard, Fort Pickens was completed in 1834. It was one of four forts that were never occupied by Confederate forces during the Civil War. The Battle of Santa Rosa Island in 1861 is known as the first major Civil War battle on Florida soil. After the Civil War, additional batteries and other defenses were constructed in and around the fort over the years, including cannons. The fort remained an important military post until 1947. More of its history can be discovered at http://www.exploresouthernhistory.com/santarosa.html

Another historic gem about Fort Pickens is that it was used as a prison for Geronimo and a handful of Apaches after the Civil War. He became a tourist attraction until he was imprisoned elsewhere. Take a tour and enjoy some interesting American history and be sure to bring your camera. To learn more about the attraction before you visit, check out their site at http://www.nps.gov/guis/planyourvisit/fort-pickens.htm.

Looking for some family fun in the sun? Located in the heart of Pensacola is a kid's paradise known as Sam's Fun City. This mecca of major fun has two parks: Surf City and Fun City. Surf City has twelve water slides, a 1,200 ft. lazy river, and a junior activity pool. Lockers are available to rent for the day.

If it's lasers and lights you are looking for, check out Fun City with the best laser tag arena Pensacola has to offer. They also have a new arcade room that has fifty exciting games to play. Come inside their three-story play zone that houses huge inflatable play structures and other super fun activities. Still not enough? No problem. Fun City also has bumper boats and Hollywood miniature golf. Go for a ride at one of their go-kart tracks. There's a track for the little ones and another one for the not-so-little ones. If all this fun makes you hungry, you can fill your tanks at Bullwinkle's Family Food 'n

Fun located in the arcade, with a menu of pizza, burgers, hot dogs, salads, and sandwiches. For more information visit http://www.samsfuncity.com for a complete list of rides, prices, directions and hours of operation.

Have a great time in the city of Pensacola where you'll discover combat science and technology at the Pensacola Naval Air Museum. Located roughly thirty-five minutes from the beach, it offers an interesting trip through our nation's aviation history. The museum offers free guided as well as self-guided tours, an IMAX theater, café, and store. The famous Blue Angels are there every Wednesday to sign autographs. (Please check website for specific details.) The museum contains numerous exhibits and collections. Kids and adults alike will enjoy climbing inside a cockpit and flipping switches as they imagine themselves flying off into the wild blue yonder. Enjoy a stroll through history as you tour the museum's Home Front U.S.A.; a fascinating stroll through the typical small town Main Street during World War II. Check their website at http://www.navalaviationmuseum.org.

From the blue waters of the gulf to the emerald green of a four-leaf clover, McGuire's Irish Pub and Brewery, located at 600 E. Gregory St. in Pensacola, will get your spirits in an Irish state of mind. Famous for its steaks and burgers, McGuire's also offers ale from its own brewery. Enjoy a laugh and a song while you enjoy your delicious food in a festive atmosphere. You won't leave until you kiss the moose and leave a dollar on the wall (if you can find a spot). Oh, you'll be humming Danny Boy all the way home. Become an Irishman for the night and enjoy one of Pensacola's best restaurants for food and fun. Visit their website at http://www.mcguiresirishpub.com.

Feel like going wild in Florida? Look no further than the Gulf Breeze Zoo located just twenty minutes away from the beach. This is a fifty-acre facility full of animals from around the world. Enjoy feeding the giraffes (but watch out for those tongues!) and walk around the Australian Free-Flight Budgiery as colorful parakeets fly around, sometimes perching on your hand to eat treats. Stroll along the walkways and see big cats, primates, bears and more. Enjoy a train ride through a thirty-acre preserve where zebras, rhinoceros, deer and antelope roam free. For more information about directions, hours and prices please visit http://www.gulfbreezezoo.org.

A good idea before you book your trip to Pensacola Beach is to check for the numerous local events and festivals, including Mardi Gras, the Gulf Coast Renaissance Faire, Pensacola JazzFest, Blue Angels air shows, and the Pensacola State Fair. The Gulf Coast is known for its artists and has many arts and craft shows that offer various works of art from amazing paintings to unique handmade furniture. A list of upcoming events can be found at http://www.visitpensacola.com/landing/events-festivals.

Though Pensacola Beach is shoreline entertainment, shopping, and dining at its best, the beaches are what people really come to enjoy. The crystal clear waters soothe, the sugar white sand delights, and the beautiful sunrises and sunsets paint the sky in colors that will inspire you. Come unwind, become a kid again, search for seashells, build sandcastles, let the water soothe your soul, and watch dolphins swim and play out in the Gulf. Stroll along the beach at the edge of the water and let it wash away your stress and worries. The air is fresh with the smell of sea and salt. Here you will find peace, beauty, tranquility, great cuisine, history and fun.

Visit Pensacola Beach
http://www.visitpensacola.com/landing/pensacola-beach
Directions: Interstate 10 to I-110. South to the city. Follow directions to the beach on Hwy 98 to Pensacola Beach Road.

Sun, Surf, Sand, and Serenity on Dauphin Island, Alabama

Marilyn Johnston – Mobile, AL

When your Gulf Coast vacation days are filled to the brim with running here, seeing that, spending an hour here and an hour there, the sugar white sands of Dauphin Island beckon you to pull up a beach chair and sit a spell. Rest and restore body and soul in a relaxed, natural setting—Dauphin Island, Alabama.

Dauphin Island is a pearlescent gem in the Gulf of Mexico. A barrier island off the mouth of Mobile Bay, the island's beaches and family-oriented attractions offer a quiet respite from the hustle and bustle of large, crowded venues. The island is easily accessible by the 3.3-mile high-rise bridge that replaced the original drawbridge destroyed by Hurricane Frederick in 1979. You can also reach the island by boat (there are numerous boat launch sites) and a ferry.

Not just an island getaway, Dauphin Island is rich in history dating back to the Mississippian Indian Era. Centuries later, the island played an important part in the birthing of the United States as a nation.

Shell Mound Park is located on the island's north shore. Archeologists date the oyster shell mounds to as far back as A.D. 1100-1500. Over time, the island's forests have reclaimed the mounds, and there is an oak tree in today's eleven-acre Shell Mound Park thought to be more than 800 years old. At that age, the tree witnessed the arrival of French settlers, the American Revolution, and the Civil War.

In 1707, the French explorer Pierre LeMoyne de'Iberville christened the French island colony "Dauphine," in honor of the heir to the French throne. The island was also the designated capitol of the Louisiana Territory, which, at that time, comprised almost two-thirds of the United States.

More than a century later, Dauphin Island and the waters surrounding the little strip of land played a now-famous role in the Civil War. In 1862, the City of Mobile became the Confederacy's primary port in the eastern Gulf of Mexico. On the east end of Dauphin Island, which lies forty miles south of Mobile, sat the brand-new Fort Gaines (completed in 1861). Across the bay from Fort Gaines was Fort Morgan, built on a spit of mainland that is now Gulf Shores, Alabama. The twenty-six cannons of Fort Gaines and the forty-six guns of Fort Morgan guarded the main channel into Mobile Bay, which the Confederacy had mined (called torpedoes). It was during the Union Navy's assault on Mobile Bay in 1864 that Union Admiral David Farragut lashed his fourteen wooden ships together in pairs and is said to have given his famous command, "Damn the torpedoes, full speed ahead!" With that, Farragut sent his vessels, under full sail, into the mined channel.

Fort Gaines served the nation in World War II as well when the U.S. Coast Guard was stationed there to patrol Gulf Coast waters in search of prowling enemy submarines looking for merchant ships to sink. By some counts, as many as 20 U-boats ventured into the Gulf of Mexico during 1942 and 1943.

Historic Fort Gaines is now on the list of "America's Eleven Most Endangered Historic Places." Topmost among the Fort's threats is the erosion of its Gulf of Mexico shoreline. The structure and museum are open to tourists, including tours and historical reenactment events. Civil War buffs will delight in seeing the anchor from Admiral Farragut's flagship, the *USS Hartford*, as well as some of the original cannons used in the Battle of Mobile Bay. There are pre-Civil War buildings to explore, an operational blacksmith shop, and tunnel systems to the fortified corner bastions.

Near Fort Gaines, the Dauphin Island Sea Lab is home for the State of Alabama's Marine Environmental Sciences Consortium, an organization comprised of several of Alabama's colleges and universities for the purpose of providing educational programs in marine sciences. There, studies of the 2010 oil spill showed how the Gulf's fish, crabs, and shrimp all rebounded. The Sea Lab's front-line observations of that near disaster led them to identify a need for ongoing scientific infrastructure and monitoring programs to ensure the future health and productivity of our coastal waters.

The Estuarium at the Consortium showcases the four key habitats of coastal Alabama; the Barrier Islands, the Mobile Tensaw River Delta, the Northern Gulf of Mexico, and Mobile Bay—the fourth largest estuary system in the United States. The Billy Goat Hole Gallery in the Estuarium features a replica of an old French sailing vessel called the Discovery Ship. Saltwater tanks in the Gulf of Mexico Gallery contain octopi, lobsters, eels, seahorses, sharks, horseshoe crabs, blue crabs, and jellyfish.

In addition to the 10,000-square-foot exhibit hall, the facility has a Living Marsh Boardwalk that offers island visitors an up-close and personal look at the plants and animals found in the surrounding marine habitats. The Sea Lab's mission is cutting edge marine research, K-to-Gray Education, and community service. You can participate by buying a plaque with your name, your family name, or a loved one's, and have it permanently displayed on the Boardwalk.

A beach, dunes, and forest excursion will walk you through the Audubon Bird Sanctuary's maritime forest where you'll see longleaf and slash pine, magnificent live oak, Southern magnolia, and Tupelo gum trees. The excursion continues on to the dunes and the beach. The graceful plumes of sea oats that wave over the dunes provide lovely scenic settings for photographers as well as protective cover for small critters. Look for the worms that live in the beach sand and the clams that use water jets to burrow.

Each summer, "Share the Beach" volunteers search the sands of Dauphin Island for the nests of endangered sea turtles. Virtually twenty-four hours a day when hatching time is near (some of the hatchlings like to arrive in the wee hours of the morning), these volunteers walk the beaches to locate the nests, and then monitor and protect them and the hatchlings from natural and human dangers. Volunteers also lead tours and talk to school groups about the sea turtles and Alabama's coastal ecosystem. Since 2003, an estimated 28,300 hatchlings have safely entered the waters of the Gulf of Mexico. During the 2010 season, the U.S. Fish and Wildlife Service determined that it was too dangerous for hatchlings to enter the Gulf waters until more of the Deep Water Horizon oil spill was cleaned away, so the turtle eggs were transported to Cape Canaveral, Florida, for release into the Atlantic.

Contact adopt1@alabamaseaturtles.com if you'd like to learn more about "Share the Beach" sea turtle conservation and the sea turtle nesting season. And if you're visiting a Gulf Coast beach and see a "crawl line" that leads to the water, or, sadly, if you find a vandalized turtle egg nest, you're encouraged to report it.

Because of Dauphin Island's unique location—it's on the flyway of spring and fall bird migrations—the entire island is designated as a bird sanctuary. The island is the first landfall for exhausted birds making their way across the Gulf from Central and South America each spring. Conversely, each fall, Dauphin Island is the last port of call for the feathered travelers, where they rest and feed before embarking on their long flight home. Thousands of birders arrive each year to see and photograph the annual migrations. A fresh water lake, Gulf beaches, swamp, pine forest, and dunes are all part of the 164-acre Audubon Bird Sanctuary, located on the eastern end of the island.

Dauphin Island is also home to the Alabama Coastal Birding Trail. Nature interpretive signs are placed strategically along the paths to aid visitors along the way. The trail system includes a 1,000-foot handicap accessible boardwalk that begins at the parking lot. The boardwalk takes visitors to Gaillard Lake that sits at the southern edge of the piney woods. Approximately four and a half acres in size, Gaillard Lake is bordered on two sides by pine trees and abuts the Tupelo Swamp on its east and south borders. There is a raised walkway to follow through the Tupelo Swamp from which you might even spot an alligator or two.

When you're ready for an off-island excursion, tour the beautiful Bellingrath Gardens in nearby Theodore, Alabama, where brilliantly colored flora and fauna abound year-round. Visit the fishing villages of Coden and Bayou La Batre, and enjoy fresh, off-the-boat seafood. Head over to the Mobile Bay Ferry on the east end of the island for a safe and scenic ferry ride to Fort Morgan and Gulf Shores, AL. The "Fort Morgan" and "Marissa Mae Nicole" ferries connect Fort Gaines on Dauphin Island to Fort Morgan, two of the Gulf Coast's historic landmarks.

Visitors can join the permanent residents—there are about 1,300 of them—and drop a line in the water at one of the fishing piers that provide access to the Gulf of Mexico and the Mississippi Sound. Deep water fishing enthusiasts will want to hop aboard one of the charter boats to spend a few hours on an exciting game fishing expedition.

The Alabama Deep Sea Fishing Rodeo takes place on Dauphin

Island every July. The three-day event attracts thousands of anglers annually and offers prize packages totaling more than $400,000 The Rodeo is a charity-driven event that donates all profits to the University of South Alabama's Department of Marine Sciences and annually funds academic scholarships. Cancelled in 2010 because of the BP oil spill, the Alabama Deep Sea Fishing Rodeo returned to its schedule in 2011, and the lure of fishing for forty-pound-plus king mackerel or tiger sharks that tip the scales at more than 260 pounds proved irresistible to fisherman from around the country. So many anglers showed up for a shot at the prize money that Guinness World Records designated the 2011 Rodeo as the largest fishing tournament in the world.

The island's population swells during November, December January, and February, when snowbirds arrive from frosty northern climes. The Dauphin Island Campground is a favorite site. Also popular are vacation home rentals where you can enjoy breakfast on the porch of a beachfront cottage with stunning views of the Gulf of Mexico. Most cottages have space to sleep up to ten people or more—bring the whole family. There are also condominium rental with fresh-water swimming pools.

When the traditional winter Holiday Season is over, Islanders and visitors look forward to Mardi Gras celebrations—which around the Gulf Coast is a season, not just a day. Dauphin Island's Krewe De La Dauphine takes pride in being first on the parade schedule and kicks off the season with a celebratory procession down Bienville Boulevard. If Lent begins in early February, as it did in 2013, the Krewe De La Dauphine is on the road in early January. Mardi Gras which means Fat Tuesday, is the last day of the carnival season before certain followers of the Christian faith begin fasting for Lent which starts on Ash Wednesday.

Other community events drawing visitors to the island are the cooking competitions. There's a Chili Cook-Off, a Wings and Waves chicken wing cook-off, and the Dauphin Island Gumbo Festival. The Gumbo Festival comes complete with musical bands that take to the stage throughout the three-day weekend in March Cooking teams from around the country recreate their best recipes to compete for prizes and the bragging rights of making the best pot of "Seafood Gumbo" or "Freestyle Gumbo." The 2012 event served more than 100 gallons of seafood gumbo to visitors.

There are family-friendly restaurants, a diet-busting bakery offering carryout food, and a delightful souvenir shop. Four churches provide regular Sunday and midweek services welcoming sandal-footed worshipers and visitors of all religions.

Dauphin Island is less than twenty miles long, and ambitious visitors find it just about perfect for canoeing, kayaking, or a leisurely morning or afternoon bicycle ride. Beachcombers, surfers, swimmers, and sun worshipers dot the white sand beaches where colorful kites dance on Gulf breezes in the blue sky above.

So, y'all come on down and stop awhile. Sip a sweet tea and bite into some deliciously fresh seafood. Dauphin Island, Alabama, is a family resort vacation destination chockfull of laidback Southern hospitality. As the Dauphin Island Chamber of Commerce says, "Discover Dauphin Island … it's how real family vacations used to be."

Dauphin Island
Directions: From Interstate 10, take Hwy 193 (Dauphin Island Parkway) south for about thirty miles.
http://www.dauphinisland.org

Walking the T

Fowler McLain – Ocean Springs, MS

Writers recount hometown experiences, good or bad, with obvious sincerity. I write about Ocean Springs, my chosen hometown, with sincere contentment, pride, and more than a little bit of gloating. After all, it's not considered bragging if it's all true. Ocean Springs is a quaint, picturesque, quiet, historic artist's colony nestled between Ft. Bayou and the Mississippi Sound, fast-paced Biloxi and industrial Pascagoula, and the Katrina ravaged, but resilient beach and U.S. Highway 90.

Ocean Springs was founded as Ft. Maurepas in 1699 by Pierre le Moyne D'Iberville of France and served as the capital of the Louisiana Territory. After the discovery of mineral springs in the 1850's, sanitariums were built and the beautification that would become a lasting part of the town's heritage began with the planting of Live oaks. These oaks, deliberately tilted, still shade downtown streets and walkways.

If you are traveling Highway 90, the scenic Gulf Coast route, Ocean Springs is just a blip on the radar. Commerce on the highway is much the same as commerce everywhere, lined with chain grocery stores, all the top fast-food outlets, gas stations, and Walmart. Missing are sky blocking billboards and an excess of high-rise buildings. The only two such buildings are retirement centers, which, at seven stories, are only tall by Ocean Springs'

standards. Ocean Springs has eight official historic districts, but today we explore the downtown area where Government Street ends at Washington Avenue. We locals call it "Walking the T."

Beneath the brick tower at the corner of 90 and Washington, the restored L&N depot lures train enthusiasts, the curious, and young adventurers alike. The rail line was completed in 1870 by the New Orleans, Mobile & Chattanooga Railroad and taken over by the L&N a decade later. Ocean Springs became a retreat for the elite of New Orleans and Mobile who came for the mineral springs or were running from the yellow fever epidemics. At the station, it's easy to visualize a steamer pulling in amid noise and smoke to let off its passengers.

On Saturday a farmer's market is in full swing at Depot Plaza. Passalong plants are for sale in disposable drinking cups along with spring vegetables and tomatoes, juicy red for salads or green for frying. Jars of honey, pickled Cajun okra, and pepper-jelly line card tables beneath canvas canopies. Under a coloring book blue sky, with tee shirt temperatures, the atmosphere is a laidback kind of festive. Prices are reasonable and gardening advice is free. Across the street in Marshall Park, commissioned by the city in 1911, a variety of flowers are in bloom. The original bandstand is spruced up and ready for the next concert.

The depot now houses the Realizations Art Gallery and the Chamber of Commerce Visitor Center, where walking maps are available. Run by the multigenerational multitalented Anderson family, it is warm, user friendly, and as much about history as art. In the late 1920s the original three Anderson brothers, Peter, Walter, and James, opened Shearwater Pottery, located at 102 Shearwater Dr. (228) 875-7320, and it is still operational despite Hurricane Katrina's efforts to shut it down. The next generation continues to produce the whimsical figurines, unique dinnerware and decorative tiles that brought national attention to the growing reputation of Ocean Springs as an artist colony. The world famous Walter Anderson Museum of Art, 510 Washington Ave., (228) 872-3164, offers an incredible spectrum of the famous artist's modern/transitional/naturalistic art, including his distinctive oil paintings, watercolors, ceramics, and wooden sculptures.

Today there are at least six other galleries in the T area: The

Pink Rooster, Theresa's Gallery, The Art House, Local Color Gallery, Gina's Antiques, Arts, and Gifts, and Ivey Framing and Gallery. Moran's Art Studio is within walking distance for those brave enough to cross Highway 90. Their wares run from upscale and expensive to down-home and affordable. Paintings, sculpture, local crafts, and photography, classic, provocative, and quirky, they all have a home here, along with the artists themselves. In every place, whatever the price range, the work is exceptional, the people welcoming and knowledgeable, and not the least condescending to a fine arts novice, like me.

At the base of the T, the Mary C. O'Keefe Cultural Center of Arts and Education, 1600 Government St. (228) 818-2878, is the perfect place to upgrade that novice status. Fittingly housed in a restored 1927 schoolhouse, the nonprofit center offers classes in traditional art forms and the not-so traditional ones, including performing arts, language skills, culinary, jewelry making, pottery, woodwork, and photography. Dramas and musicals play out in the theater as well as concerts from bluegrass to big band, and community meetings.

Washington Avenue has been called "a street out-of-time," and at first glance, the description fits. Cyclists and walkers have the right of way by tradition, not signs. In fact, signs are again notable by their discretion; nothing blinking at you, no neon and no plastic. A few old style, freestanding chalkboards with handwritten messages dot the sidewalk along with decorative shrubs, flowerpots, and benches. A wooden rocker completes the illusion. But unlike Mayberry, this city stands firmly in the 21st century. The old oaks carry their age with dignity, shading the SUV's and bicycles with the same care they once gave horses and Model-T's. Unhurried walkers of all ages are wearing shorts and tank tops, flip-flops and Reeboks. Parasols and top hats have been replaced by ball caps. Endearing as the peaceful past seems, these modern touches bode well for air conditioned exploring.

Wonderful craft and variety shops blend into each other, refusing to be classified. Regional souvenirs yes, but not one clichéd *Mississippi Redneck* tee shirt, no bumper stickers made in China, no suggestive jokes on key chains or corny puns on miniature outhouses. Within one block you can find things you never expected and things you never imagined. Tchotchkes, chintzy and classy hang on driftwood, weathered sections of slatted doors, as well as modern wire stands. Christmas and Mardi Gras are celebrated year round. Colorful Anderson prints and motifs are abundant as well as the fleur de lis of the beloved New Orleans Saints. Like the galleries themselves, everyone inside is friendly and informative. You'll be offered coffee, as a guest not a customer, and have all your questions answered, even the dumb ones. "Why would anyone buy an old washtub?" They make great planters. "Does Squirrel-Away really work?" You'll soon find out.

Cleverly placed among this magical kingdom are the businesses of everyday life. Subtle dignified signs on small architecturally-fitting offices blend in gracefully. In the T, lawyers really do hang out their shingles. Clarence Darrow or Ben Matlock moseying to work in a spiffy seersucker suit would have been right at home. Within a block you can cash a check, buy a house, get a haircut, or get a tooth filled.

Ladies' boutiques run from young and hip to chic and sexy, to breezy and comfortable. In an art gallery, you'll find one-of-a-kind dramatic period dresses worthy of Zelda Fitzgerald, being sold by a real live Julia Sugarbaker. Menswear is available too. Guys, as stereotypical as it sounds, just don't find as much pleasure shopping for it. If you need jeans, they're there. If you need water shoes and swim trunks, they're there. God forbid, you need a tux, it's there, too. No fuss, no hassle, and no time wasted going to a mall.

Time saved can be time spent in the fun places. For dog lovers there's nothing closer to heaven than a pet supplies shop. Sent to Two Dogs Dancing, 619A Washington Ave. (228) 875-0150, for an emergency squeaky frog replacement, I came away with princess dresses for my four-legged princesses and a collar that said "Dog" – to differentiate my writing partner's baby girl from a horse.

A friend's grandchild's fourth birthday deserves better than Walmart. Such an event calls for a real toy store and another blissful hour in Miners Toys at 927 Washington Ave. (228) 875-8697. Toy decisions can't be rushed. Sock puppets and stick horses bring back memories of my early childhood. Star Wars blasters and model trains raise memories of my second one. Dolls, collectable and huggable, smile their welcome. They even have potholder looms and local writers' books.

New in town, Kajun Kubbard, 1000 Government St., Suite B (228) 215-1203, qualifies as a man's toy store. It has the real good stuff: favorite team paraphernalia, a stockpot you could bathe in, pirogue shaped ice buckets big enough for a Super Bowl party, but too big to carry all the way back to my truck. The beignet and king cake mixes I did carry home came with instructions simple enough for me, but my wife is still trying to figure out what to do with wild game seasoning.

At five in the morning, you can get a doughnut made out of potatoes, a Germanic concept and well-guarded secret recipe (Tato-Nut Donut Shop – 1114 Government St.). Another T bakery (French Kiss Pastries – 837 Howard Ave.) has cannoli, an Italian classic, but these have to come from Heaven. Ham and eggs, grits and gravy, sausage and biscuits, Bloody Marys and Mimosas for the daring or hung-over – it's all here, served with a great view and good company. The only thing you won't find in the T is a bad cup of coffee, though I'm forced to admit the Lebanese blend (Phoenicia Gourmet Restaurant – 1223 Government St. (228) 875-0603) is too tough for me, and the chicory makes me sneeze.

For lunch or dinner we have the choice of crepes or tapas, a New York Reuben, a New Orleans po-boy, sushi, or wood-fired pizza, even vegan or vegetarian. A dedicated carnivore, I'm not sure of the difference. There's Southern comfort, Cajun spicy, and Phoenicia, a classy Greek-Lebanese family friendly restaurant where you can get Baba Ghanuj, seafood gumbo, and a shrimp fajita in the same meal.

For the time-capsule-experience lunch, you must take the step back in time to Lovelace Drugs, 801 Washington Ave. (228) 875-4272. The brick building proudly announces its age with its architectural style and Coca-Cola logo on the side. Predating city ordinances, predating a lot of the city, the building flaunts its sassy swinging neon sign. Neighborhood drugstores are rapidly going the way of full service gas stations, but Lovelace is not a museum mockup honoring their passing. A busy full service pharmacy, they offer money orders, parcel service drops and delivery service to the retirement homes. Drugstore typical sundries share shelf space with the T's atypical specialties, Coca-Cola memorabilia, "Cruising the Coast" tee shirts and sweaters, and bottles of national acclaimed locally produced barbeque sauce. Lovelace's soda counter, the type made popular in the 1930's, has all the soda and ice cream delights of its predecessors as well as sandwiches and snacks. Vinyl stools and café tables, not rickety enough to be original, but authentic in appearance are situated, so you can enjoy a simple lunch, a decadent dessert, and watch the people parade. Lovelace even has its own label of bottled cream soda.

Henrietta's Café is another shrine to local history. At 1013 Government, near the intersection with Washington, it first opened in 1943. Henrietta Savage served the boys leaving for World War II and hosted their return celebrations. For the next fifty years the rapidly changing world was hashed out at the never changing Henrietta's. Rumor has it more business and political deals were cut over their sweet tea and fried mullet than in any law office in the South. Henrietta's closed in 1995, and the several businesses that occupied the building avoided the wrath of townspeople by keeping the hand-painted sign at the front of the cafe. A good thing, as the fates would have it, as the café is to be reopened by Henrietta's grandchildren, restored as originally as possible. I plan to be first in line when it does.

Love the nightlife, got to boogie. Don your dancing shoes and hit Government Street about dark thirty. Music and laughter play to the street while you pick your scene. Mosaic Tapas Bar (1010 Government St.) near the T and Mezo's Juke Joint (1911 Government St.) just east of the Mary C are some of the places where the young and young at heart mingle and dance until the wee hours. Several others offer televisions for those with money on the game and prefer their feet propped up. Sedate background music doesn't interfere with conversation, last minute bets, or referee bashing. Al Fresco's outdoor patio (708 Washington Ave.) is ideal for stargazers and people watchers. Comfortable cozy neighborhood bars, such as Manhattan Grill (705 Washington Ave.) welcome regulars by name and have your favorite brew in your hand before you even decide on a seat. Not a dive in the bunch and there's Guinness on tap, a personal favorite. If you're lucky enough to be here for St. Patrick's Day, an annual pub-crawl lets you scope them all out in their community party best.

Community parties are the rule rather than the exception in Ocean Springs. The T frequently closes its streets to vehicle traffic for festivals and fairs. Along with St. Patrick's Day, there is the Peter Anderson celebration of the arts the first weekend in November and the Food and Wine Festival in mid-May. The annual Herb and Garden festival welcomes spring and the Landing of D'Iberville is reenacted every year with great pageantry and ceremony. Mardi Gras parades, Christmas parades, and Cruising the Coast are also yearly events.

What separates Ocean Springs from other time-capsule towns is its vibrancy, modern sensibilities, and fresh outlook. It deserves a full book, a chapter for each of the historical districts and one just for the people. Once I was the tourist passing through. Enchanted by what I found, I came back to stay. Now I take pride in being part of the welcome committee for the National Trust for Historic Preservations the 2013 winner of the Great American Main Street Award.

Downtown Ocean Springs, Mississippi
http://oceanspringschamber.com
Directions: I-10. Take the Oceans Springs Exit, Hwy 609. Cross Hwy 90 and reach the "T" in 3 blocks.

Welcome to Biloxi

Judy Davies - Gautier, MS

The Lighthouse

Steadfast watch I stand.
Katrina could not move me,
The Gulf Coast is mine.

The only lighthouse to stand in the middle of a four-lane highway, the Biloxi Lighthouse bids a warm welcome to sunbathers, boaters and tourists to Mississippi's Gulf Coast.

In March of 1847, a $12,000 appropriation by Congress led to the erection of the Biloxi Lighthouse on a one-acre tract of land purchased from John Fayard for $600.00. The prominent landmark was erected in 1848 and was the first lighthouse in the South to be fashioned of cast-iron. Its original lighting consisted of nine lamps and fourteen-inch reflectors, replaced in 1856 by a fourth-order Fresnel lens. Although more than ten lighthouses had been originally built to delineate the Mississippi coastline, when Hurricane Georges toppled the masonry tower at Round Island in 1998, it left the Biloxi Lighthouse as the only remaining lighthouse standing along the Gulf Coast.

In 1948 Marcellus Howard became the first keeper of the lighthouse. Civilians operated the Biloxi Lighthouse from 1848 to 1939, including several female lightkeepers beginning with Mary Reynolds from 1854 to 1866. During the Civil War, a group of "Home Guards" removed her from her duties, seizing the keys to the tower and ordered the light extinguished. Caring for several orphaned children, Ms. Reynolds petitioned the Mississippi governor, who retained her at her post until after the war ended, all the way to 1866.

Following the war, the lighthouse was restored from its damage in which a portion of the wall had collapsed allowing the tower to lean approximately two feet from its vertical position. Had the iron sheath not been in place, the entire structure likely would have collapsed. The structure was righted to its previous vertical position during the 1866 reconstruction and a fifth-order Fresnel lens installed. During this time, Peter Younghans had been appointed lightkeeper. When he passed away during his first year as keeper, his wife Maria assumed the responsibility for the light and tended it faithfully, sending out its guiding beam regardless of weather for over fifty years. When she retired in 1918, her daughter, Miranda, who had previously assisted her mother, was promoted to keeper of the light, a position she retained until her retirement in 1929. The light was electrified in 1926.

In 1880 the dilapidated lighthouse keeper's quarters were torn down and a new facility constructed. A 900-foot wharf with boat davits at its outer end was built in 1902 and in 1906 the station's cisterns were removed and the quarters connected to municipal waterworks. The U.S. Coast Guard assumed responsibility for the light in 1939, eventually declaring it to be "surplus property" and deeding it to the City of Biloxi, who opened it for public tours. In 1940, with the retirement of lighthouse keeper Joseph Olivier, the light was automated. The City of Biloxi acquired the lightkeeper's residence in 1941 for $1,200.00 to use for its Chamber of Commerce. That facility was destroyed in 1969 by Hurricane Camille.

Today the Biloxi lighthouse stands not only as a welcoming sight along the city's beachfront, but as a reminder post-Katrina of a city that refuses to be toppled, despite being battered by numerous storms. The lighthouse stood through Katrina, though not without significant damage. The sixty-four-foot tall structure lost many of its bricks along the interior of the cast-iron structure along with its electrical system and the windows in its cupola. Soon after Katrina, an American flag was draped from the top of the lighthouse, a testimony to the resilience of Biloxi's residents, whose resoluteness has often been tested by hurricane winds. Their resolve to face and surmount the challenges of hurricane seasons remains firm. FEMA and MEMA provided funds for the restoration of this historical coastal landmark at a cost of $400,000 and fourteen months of work under the tutelage of Biloxi contractor, J. O. Collins.

In 2009 the City of Biloxi and the United States Postal Service joined forces to pay tribute to this longstanding symbol, the most photographed landmark on Mississippi's Gulf Coast, with the issue of a postage stamp commemorating the Biloxi Lighthouse. The Lighthouse re-opened its doors to the public in March of 2010. Guided tours are available with reservations required for group tours. The Biloxi Tour Train offers a 90-minute tour of historical Biloxi beginning at perhaps Biloxi's most notable location—the Biloxi Lighthouse.

There is much more that Biloxi has to offer in addition to its lighthouse. The Saenger Theater of Biloxi originally opened on January 13, 1930 at its present location on Reynoir Street. The 1500-seat theater housed dressing rooms and stage facilities to accommodate vaudeville and traveling shows as well as equipment for presenting early sound films. The Saenger was deeded to the City of Biloxi in 1995 and the theater underwent a major restoration lasting eight years with the dramatic improvements unveiled in November of 2003. The Saenger has been home to the Gulf Coast Symphony Orchestra, dance troupes and local theater companies. Damage from Hurricane Katrina forced numerous additional repairs to the facility and cooperative efforts from the community to relocate performances while repairs were made. Today, the Saenger Theater serves as home to the symphony as well as a stage for plays, concerts, and many other performing arts. The Saenger is surrounded by several small art galleries, specialty shops, and small cafe's that will delight your senses.

The Parks and Recreation Department of Biloxi offers a variety of recreational options for visitors including parks, playgrounds, athletic fields, walking tracks, tennis and basketball courts, a community center, senior center, and the Biloxi Natatorium. The Town Green on Beach Boulevard provides space for celebrations and programs and may be reserved for special events by local organizations.

Biloxi's Edgewater Mall provides readily available shopping. Here, tourists will find a wide variety of stores from which to choose. Approximately 100 stores offer everything imaginable to make your trip to the mall a fruitful shopping experience. Since Edgewater Mall is across the street from the beach, swing through the mall's food court or stop at a nearby fast food location, and then walk across the street to the beach where you can enjoy your lunch along with an unobstructed view of the Gulf. Just north of the railroad tracks of Edgewater Drive, Biloxi's Center Stage Theater entertains visitors with some of the best in Community Theater, attesting to the fact that there is a lot of very fine talent on the Coast. Come enjoy one of their productions and see for yourself!

Probably few things in Biloxi are as visible as its casinos. Biloxi is home to eight casinos, most of which line Beach Boulevard (Highway 90). Adding to an already sizable beachfront, the casinos offer Gulf-view hotel rooms from comfortable and stylish to stunning and romantic, restaurants ranging from casual coffee shops to elegant fine dining, and headliner entertainment with a variety of shows. Jimmy Buffet's "Margaritaville" is the newest of the casinos, opened in May of 2012. The Golden Nugget, Palace Casino, Hard Rock, IP Casino, Treasure Bay, The Grand Casino, and the very elaborate Beau Rivage provide anything and everything the tourist could ask for from valet and babysitting services to nightclubs, shopping, buffets, spas, salons, gambling, golf packages and more.

Many fine restaurants call Biloxi home. Mary Mahoney's at 110 Rue Magnolia, is one of the oldest, a stalwart of Southern

Mississippi cuisine, specializing in seafood fare and fine wines. Jazzeppi's at 195 Porter Ave is a locals' favorite for Italian, with veal served in four different styles. Newer restaurants include Half Shell Oyster House at 125 Lameuse St., locally owned and featuring, yes, oysters on the half shell - raw, grilled, or a local favorite, oysters Bienville, New Orleans style. Shaggy's, at 1763 Beach Blvd., is another locally owned spot. Built on the beach side, its Caribbean style décor invites patrons to relax and enjoy the open window sea breezes as they dine on seafood freshly caught from the Gulf.

Last, let's not forget the beautiful beach itself. Come to Biloxi, kick off your shoes, slip your feet into the warm sand, enjoy a lazy day of swimming and surfing, or plan a day of deep sea fishing from one of Biloxi's charter vessels where you'll find some spectacular offshore fishing. Come visit Biloxi. You'll be glad you did!

The Biloxi Lighthouse is located in the middle of U.S. 90 at Porter Avenue, south of the Biloxi Visitor's Center and just west of the I-110 loop and the Beau Rivage Resort and Casino. The Biloxi museum's office can be reached by email at museums@biloxi.ms.us or by phone

Biloxi, MS http://www.biloxi.ms.us
Directions: I-10 to I-110. South to Hwy 90, and exit East. The Biloxi Lighthouse is located in the middle of U.S. 90 at Porter Avenue, south of the Biloxi Visitor's Center and just west of the I-110 loop. The Biloxi museum's office can be reached by mail at museums@biloxi.ms.us or by phone at 228-374-3105. Admission is $5.00 for adults, $2.00 for students with discounts available for groups.

Traveling the Coast Road

Sue Monkress – Gulfport, MS

The Mississippi Gulf Coast, an area steeped in history and beauty, abounds in appealing places and activities to explore: from abundant lively musical and artistic events to tours of historical buildings and museums, to nautical outings – fishing charters, boating and family water recreation. To help first-time visitors select from the myriad bounty of enjoyment, simply meandering down Highway 90, also called "Beach Boulevard," is wonderful entertainment.

Of the State's one-hundred-mile southern border, Highway 90 hugs nearly thirty gorgeous miles of beach coast. From sweeping views over the bridges of Biloxi Bay on the east to the Bay of St. Louis on the west, visitors will travel past clear gulf waters mirroring the current mood of the skies bordered by glistening white beaches and gracefully swaying sea grass. The journey provides idyllic scenes of boating, historic houses, and centuries-old live oaks framing the road like lacy curtains. From Beauvoir, Jefferson Davis' antebellum home in Biloxi, on westward toward the cities of Pass Christian and Bay St. Louis, visitors will be transported to another era, awed by the beauty and resilience of magnificent trees surrounding the elegant Southern architecture of coast homes. Even oaks that didn't survive the gargantuan forces of hurricanes are preserved, carved into wonderful sculptures by local artist, Marlin Miller, to be enjoyed for miles along the coast road.

During the long mild weather summer season, beach vendors along the coast road offer rentals to visitors – two-person paddleboats, aqua cycles, kayaks, jet skis, beach chairs and umbrellas. For the more adventurous, try parasailing!

Forty-foot schooners make Gulf excursions around the shore and day trips to nearby islands. Shrimp boat captains give educational talks during tours, highlighting the catch of the day. Boat trips to nearby barrier islands (part of the Gulf National Seashore Islands, a National park) provide daylong enjoyment. In 1702 one of the barrier islands was named *Ile aux Vaisseaux* (Ship Island). It remains home to Fort Massachusetts, a fascinating Civil War-era fortification with seasonal guided tours by park rangers. The clear waters surrounding the islands are a special treat, where beach rentals are also available for a leisurely day of sunning or swimming, as dolphins play nearby.

The chain of barrier islands reduces waves, making the gentle waters on the coast beach pleasant for children to build sand castles and explore for beach treasures. Modern resting stations located along the beach highway provide showers and refreshment machines, as well as convenient bus stops for the local Transit Authority. Relax at Jones Park near the harbor in Gulfport, where children will enjoy a nautical-inspired play area.

Special activities vary from month to month but there's always *something* happening along the coast! Because King Louis XIV established a colony on the Mississippi coast in 1699, the French influence is still apparent in architecture, as well as in favorite holidays. As soon as the Christmas decorations are put away, plans begin for Mardi Gras! Visitors can check out over twenty-five family-friendly Mardi Gras parades or balls and parties in late January and February. (Note: Mardi Gras is a family-friendly celebration *all along* the Gulf Coast, not only in "Naw'leans.") Several dozen parades with many different themes and "Krewes," such as the "Little Rascals" kids' parade, roll the streets. The Krewe of Nereids, known for its secretive society, keeps their tradition alive by not revealing the names of its parade riders -- not even Queen Doris XLVI. Spectators can enjoy music and dancing or watching the merriment. Vying for "catches" of beads and treats, from a continuous line of elaborately-decorated and themed floats holding masked riders, is a treat in itself! Lively marching bands, some featuring local school students, add to the festive atmosphere.

In March/April, join a Spring Pilgrimage to tour historic

homes and buildings throughout the Mississippi Gulf Coast, with greeters dressed in period costumes. The event, hosted by the Mississippi Gulf Coast Council of Garden Clubs is free – donations appreciated. Call 228-497-1368 or 228-990-0659 for location/times and more information. Also during this time, a two-day outdoor fine arts festival is held in Pass Christian War Memorial Park. For information, call 228-234-3812.

The Memorial Day holiday at the end of May provides entertainment in the form of the Motorcycle Blowout, where thousands of motorbikes roar along the beach. Come feel the roar of the machines and the wind in your hair. A wonderful opportunity not to be missed over this holiday is attending the free Gulf Coast Symphony's "Sounds by the Sea" patriotic concert, followed by fireworks erupting and sparkling over the Gulf.

Beginning the last weekend of May, the "Blessing of the Fleet" in Biloxi is a poignant event. The Blessing festivities cover the Biloxi Gulf Coast from the beautiful Town Green with the Fais Do-Do Street Party, to the magnificent St. Michael Catholic Church (the "Church of the Fishermen") on Point Cadet. For dates and times, see:

http://biloxiblessing.com/schedule/schedule.htm

OFF THE BEATEN (GULF ROAD) PATH:

All "Lords and ladies" are welcome to wander a couple of miles north of the Coast Road in May or October, and get lost in a Renaissance Faire in Ocean Springs. High medieval adventure lies ahead, where swordsmanship, joisting, crafts, music, and more await! Featured events include a royal procession and jousting; children's activities include a magical Faerie Garden and Royal Petting Zoo. The Society for Creative Anachronism (SCA) constructs a working medieval village to instruct in the fine arts of medieval dancing and armored sword fighting. Attendees will enjoy music and demonstrations and visiting stations offering fine crafts. More information can be found for the May Faire at http://www.stjohnsoceansprings.org under Renaissance Festival. Visit http://www.oceanspringsrenfaire.com for the October Faire. Proceeds are donated to St. Jude's Research Hospital for Children. "Faire Rules: Blades must be kept sheathed and peace-tied."

Join the nation's biggest block party, "Cruisin' the Coast," for six days in early October. Thousands of oldie cars from all over the country descend upon the coast road for free viewing, parties and friendly conversation with their owners. For many, spying a certain old car revives nostalgic memories with good friends. Walk under the oaks and relive delightful past escapades as you tour wonderfully preserved "classic" cars from many decades! Visit www.gulfcoast.org for this and other car shows and events.

In December, numerous Christmas celebrations abound – parades, tours, musical concerts in churches, historical landmarks and other venues. Beauvoir hosts nightly tours with early-period crafts, train rides, caroling, hot chocolate and more. A nighttime Christmas parade of music and beautifully lit boats delights young and old at Gulfport harbor. At the conclusion of the water parade, Santa and Mrs. Claus greet the youngsters with toys.

The Mississippi Gulf Coast births an abundance of talent. Coast towns frequently host authors and artists in art-walks and other festivals, particularly on Saturdays. "First Saturday Art Market" is held monthly at the lovely Mary C. O'Keefe Cultural Center in Ocean Springs, and Bay St. Louis hosts "Second Saturday" each month from May to October, where authors, artists, and musicians congregate along Main Street, hawking their arts. Take a relaxing stroll along the oak-lined streets of these charming communities, enjoying music and conversations with local artists. Event schedules are available on many Gulf Coast websites such as http://www.gulfcoast.org/visitors.

For the more adventurous, travel the coast's bayous and swamps, feed live alligators, exhilarate on airboat rides, kayaking trips, or bike/walk through wildlife refuges. Many eco tours are available along the Coast, from Pascagoula and Gautier to Bay St. Louis. View water equipment rentals and schedules at www.gulfcoast.org. Free programs are available on weekends at the Gulf Island National Seashore in Ocean Springs. Call (228)-875-9057 for details and dates. "Celebrate the Gulf" at Pass Christian in late March is a marine education festival with hands-on exhibits for children; spectators watch free. For more information, call (228) 475-7047 or (228) 860-5634.

The lovely Biloxi Visitors Center, located across Highway 90 from the lighthouse, provides an informational video of the region.

Helpful center employees graciously assist with information on current events and activities, while visitors take in a stunning view of the Gulf from the upstairs porch. Lighthouse guided tours are given Monday through Saturday at 9, 9:15 and 9:30 a.m., weather permitting. No reservations are required, except for group tours, which can be arranged by calling (228) 374-3105. The Mississippi Gulf Coast Coliseum, at 2350 Beach Boulevard in Biloxi, hosts many headliner entertainers, as well as ice-skating and the rousing local hockey team, "Mississippi Surge." Call (228) 594-3700 for details and tickets to events.

Numerous ways to relax and enjoy the Mississippi coast are available. Those wanting to linger awhile will find an abundance of places to stay – from luxury resorts and casinos hosting headliner entertainer concerts to quaint bed and breakfasts. Even a golf course with a spectacular view of the Gulf is right along Highway 90.

The coast offers limitless other pleasures: Rock and/or Blues festivals, BBQ, and seafood or other local cuisine cook-offs, kite festivals, historical cemetery tours with actors portraying earlier-period citizens, as well as wonderful local theater in remaining historical buildings.

Wander a few miles north to the Harrison County fairgrounds, where the Annual Scottish Games and Celtic Festival occurs in November. This huge event features live music, Celtic dance workshops, children's games, parade, Scottish vendors, food, men's and women's amateur Scottish heavy athletics competitions, a medieval village and more! In addition, don't miss the Saturday Night *Ceilidh* (pronounced Kay-lee). For details, email info@highlandsandislands.org. The fairgrounds also host a re-enactment of a Civil War battle by the Sons of Confederate Veterans. Afterward, walk among the tents of the troops, visualizing the tough daily life of a Civil War soldier. For fairground schedule details, call (228) 831-3350. A moving Civil War re-enactment is also held at Jefferson Davis' home, Beauvoir, during the Fall Muster in mid-October. For the event schedule, call (228) 388-4400.

Whether your preference is the beach, boating, the arts or discovering historical places, whatever you do, be sure to drive, walk, or bike Highway 90. Stop for refreshment or seafood and other delicious local cuisine at charming restaurants with panoramic views of the Gulf. Slow down; take a leisurely stroll on the tranquil beaches to soothe your toes and discover small sea creatures; amble down piers decorated with jubilant flocks of sea birds; perhaps encounter a curious dolphin, watch some native crabbing and throw in your own casual fishing line. South Mississippians are friendly folks; guests will effortlessly find conversation, quick friends, and immerse themselves in the atmosphere of Southern hospitality. Or just park at one of the abundant benches and *breathe in* the peaceful sea air … *aaaahh!*

The Mississippi coast road ahead beckons to be enjoyed time after time. Come on down, y'all!

Hwy 90, Harrison County
Directions: Highway 90 runs across the whole state of Mississippi, and beyond in both directions. From I-10 go south on any of the main roads, such as I-110 or Hwy 49 and head south until the beach.

Henderson Point, Pass Christian, MS

Stanley Hastings – Gulfport, MS

One of the most attractive, functional, and peaceful post-Hurricane Katrina restorations, still in progress, is that of Henderson Point, the unincorporated village on the western edge of Harrison County, between Pass Christian and in Hancock County, Bay St. Louis.

According to the historic marker formerly at the site, "Henderson's Point (was) named for John Henderson, Sr., United States senator (1839-45). In 1836, along with a business partner, Henderson acquired 15,000 acres in the area and helped promote and develop Pass Christian until his death in 1857. In 1903, descendants of Senator Henderson formed the Mexican Gulf Land Company to promote Henderson's Point as a planned community."

Bordered by the Bay of St. Louis to the west and north, the Gulf of Mexico to the south, and the city of Pass Christian to the east, the area draws water lovers – fishermen, skiers, and boaters – year round. The land area of just over a mile is also an excellent resort for cyclists and walkers, many of whom go up to the Leo W. Seal, Jr., Memorial Bridge on U. S. Highway 90 across the bay to the city of Bay St. Louis.

The state of the art, high-rise bridge was named "in recognition of (Mr. Seal) for his contributions to the State of Mississippi as a philanthropist and leader in the advancement of public education, transportation, infrastructure and Gulf Coast economic development," according to the cornerstone inscription.

From the park beneath the east end of the bridge, walkers and bikers can ascend the bridge for a spectacular view. From this distance, the beachfront of the city of Bay St. Louis looks like a neat row of miniature buildings, both residential and commercial.

The historic Our Lady of the Gulf Catholic Church steeple towers over it all, between St. Stanislaus College and Our Lady Academy. Upon closer inspection, the buildings are anything but miniature, most of them restorations or replacements of pre-Katrina structures.

The walkway and bike path, on the south side of the bridge, is also home to several sculptured mile markers, created by artist Greg Moran, who was commissioned by Kent Dusson, of the consulting firm URS Corporation. Pieces of the destroyed bridge were recycled to form the shiny, bronze plates into mile marker plaques for both the bridge and walkways. The bridge won the America's Transportation Peoples Choice Award in October 2007.

"After Hurricane Katrina toppled the old bridge, all pieces had to be removed from the water below," according to Mr. Moran. "Brass bearing plates, which had provided a cushioned joinery for the massive road decks were found among the debris. I received a call from a representative of the construction firm in charge of rebuilding the bridge. He said a plan was discussed to use those old brass blocks from the destroyed bridge to cast into decorative items for the new bridge – a sort of homage and recycling project."

Locals were asked to submit artistic drawings, of which twenty-two would be chosen. "Those winning drawings would be given to me to sculpt into high relief plaques to adorn every tenth of a mile," Mr. Moran continued. "Later, a second smaller plaque was mounted beneath the larger picturesque plaque, denoting the mileage of that particular place on the bridge. Future walkers will always be aware of how far they had come and how far they had to go.

"I began by carving a wooden representation of the plaque, then molding it in rubber. Into the rubber, I poured molten wax, and allowed that to cool and harden. Removing the wax, I had a consistent representation of the plaques, all except the design within its borders.

"I set to taking each drawing chosen by the Mississippi Arts Commission in Jackson and sculpting them one at a time onto the blank wax plaque. Once the sculpting was completed, the waxes were molded into ceramic shell molds and melted out. I poured metal back into the now empty mold, allowed them to cool, and broke the molds off. Inside was a perfect metal copy of my original sculpts.

"I carefully sealed the rough spots, polished them to a beautiful sheen, and finally chemically treated or patinaed (sic.) the plaques for rich coloring. The drawings chosen are as varied as the people who live here – majestic oaks and magnolias; playful dolphins; statuesque beauty of shrimp boats. There are also beautiful moments of stillness captured in the microcosm of a single jelly fish, or the gentle blowing and bending of the wind in cattails."

After sunset, drivers traveling the bridge are treated to a colorful cascade of lights along the trail where walkers and cyclists can often still be seen.

Among fishermen we recently caught up with early one morning was Steve Allen, who drives over from Folsom, Louisiana. "Good fishing (here)," Mr. Allen said. "I have fishing licenses in both Louisiana and Mississippi, and here I've caught redfish and black trout."

Several picnic tables and wooden and wrought iron benches can be found near where Mr. Allen was fishing, along the Jourdan River. Beneath the overpass, colorful playground equipment for children can be found to the left of the parking area, near a pavilion that has timed lights for evening use. In Henderson Point Park, there is a 0.60-mile walking loop, further away from traffic. The grounds are well maintained year round.

Back toward the east, drivers approach both the two lane Sylvester Pagano bridge, then, a few feet down the road, a sign which warns drivers that the trains that cross over the railroad tracks do not blow horns when going through.

Along the stretch adjacent to the Inn by the Sea condominiums is a delightful, clean acreage of sandbar, with piers scattered here and there over the water. Several steps of high seawall can be seen.

While shells of some storm-destroyed homes still stand, and slabs will probably always be there to remind us of past storms, a number of attractive new homes, all raised or on stilts, dot the landscape.

The only present day business evident in the area is the Point Marine Lumber Company, at the corner of Bayview Drive and Highway 90, next to the east end of the Leo W. Seal, Jr., Memorial Bridge. Begun in 1969, this business is a "supplier of marine and shoreline construction materials including timbers, piling, vinyl, full cut and T&G seawall, HDG marine hardware and dock and pier accessories," according to their business card.

Further south, toward the water, Bay St. Louis fisherman, Leo Koerner, waited one morning for assistance to repair a flat tire on his boat. According to Mr. Koerner, "My family and I have gone fishing here a long time, and we've had fun catching big trout."

Near where we had this friendly conversation, is the slab of the former Annie's Restaurant on the corner of Bayview Drive and 3rd Street. Prior to Hurricane Katrina, Annie's was the centerpiece landmark here, its roots springing from a drive-in begun nearby in 1929. Having survived a fire, several hurricanes, and a van crashing through its front windows, its final nail in the coffin was Hurricane Katrina. Today it remains a slab, a block away from the Henderson Point Boat Launch.

Along the stretch of Henderson Point north of Highway 90 are more lovely residences among a wooded, more secluded area. West, just past the two-lane bridge on the corner of Bayview Drive and Livingston Drive, is the Harrison County Fire Station number 14, which serves as the local fire station. Among street names of regional interest in this area of heavy foliage are Lemoyne Road, McLauren Road, Louisiana Avenue, Poindexter Drive, and Stennis Street. The borderline entering the city of Pass Christian is less than a mile from Highway 90.

Henderson Point Park hours are 6 AM - 10 PM.

Henderson Point
https://sites.google.com/site/thepointandisles
Directions: Highway 90 at the Western Edge of Harrison County (Pass Christian)

Gulf Islands National Seashore

Sherryl LaPointe – Gulfport, MS

One of the most beautiful, most interesting, and most "user-friendly" areas in the entire Northern Mississippi Gulf Coast is Gulf Islands National Seashore. It may be the largest "tourist attraction" as regards to physical size, and it definitely has the largest variety of activities available. Part of the National Park Service, it's the largest national seashore in the United States. It includes areas in both Mississippi and Florida, stretching from Cat Island, Mississippi to Okaloosa, Florida.

Since the majority of the land areas are islands, we will take a look at these first. All of the islands off the Mississippi coast are accessible only by boat. The Mississippi barrier islands are managed by Gulf Islands National Seashore, with the exception of portions of Cat Island.

Several islands located about ten miles off the coast of Mississippi are attractions for both tourists and local residents. These islands form a chain known as the barrier islands. They are the first line of defense from Gulf storms for the Mississippi Gulf Coast. However, if no storm is in evidence, they are wonderful recreational areas. If you choose to visit any of these islands, you will have to go by boat, whether you have your own, rent one, or charter a licensed boat operator to transport you. If you choose to charter a boat, be aware that they must be approved through the National Park Service. A list is available at the web site listed at the end of this article.

The western-most island is Cat Island. Part of this island is privately owned. The western half of the island and the southern tip belongs to the National Seashore and is available for public use. If you plan to go to this island, you will want to verify that you are going to the Gulf Islands section. Be aware there are no facilities of any type. In addition to day activities, primitive camping is permitted on this island as on all the other Mississippi islands mentioned in this article except for West Ship Island. "Primitive," for those who have not experienced it, means nothing is provided; campers must take water, food, and all other necessities with them. Campers must also practice "Leave No Trace" principles which means when they leave, they must take everything back out with them in order to have as little impact on the ecosystem as possible, which includes personal and hygiene items, to preserve the area for future campers. If your camping group includes eleven or more people, you must obtain a free wilderness permit.

The next island in the chain is West Ship Island, probably the most well known of all the islands. From some time in March through late October, there is a passenger ferry between Gulfport to the island with varying schedules according to the time of year. Once on the island, restrooms, water, and limited food are available. There are also tours and exhibits during the ferryboat season. In addition to the ferryboat, you may go to this island, as to the others, by private or chartered boat.

In addition to the beaches, sand, scenery, and wildlife, Ship Island has one other feature: Fort Massachusetts. In 1814, the British used Ship Island as a rendezvous point before attacking New Orleans. As a result of this attack, Fort Massachusetts was built, as were several similar forts at vulnerable points along the United States coastlines. The Fort never had to be used to its fullest potential as the cannons were never shot, yet now it is a piece of history. It is the best kind of history, the kind that can be both seen and touched, through which one can walk and imagine those who lived and worked there. One interesting piece of the history regarding Fort Massachusetts, which visitors will want to explore, is that of the Louisiana Native Guard, especially their time on the island and at the fort during the Civil War. Another interesting historical fact is that Ship Island had a lighthouse to warn and guide ships in the area. There have been several lighthouses from the middle of the nineteenth century until 2005 when Hurricane Katrina destroyed the last lighthouse.

Eastward from West Ship Island is, not surprisingly, East Ship Island. At one time there was only one Ship Island, but over time, with the help of tides and weather, the one island became two.

The next island in the chain, Horn Island, the largest of the Mississippi islands, is designated a wilderness area with only primitive camping allowed. It hosts a ranger station. The last of the Mississippi islands is Petit Bois Island.

Gulf Islands National Seashore then moves to the Florida areas where Perdido Key and parts of Santa Rosa Island are included. They are barrier islands, as are the islands in the Mississippi section. These are both much more developed than the areas in Mississippi. There are visitors' centers, picnic areas, and campgrounds. Many areas are handicapped accessible. These areas may be reached by vehicle, since they are connected to land by bridges and are connected by road along the length of the island.

Perdido Key is a largely undeveloped area, but does have a paved road. Primitive camping is allowed but must be at least a half mile beyond the end of the road. A free wilderness permit must be obtained at the entrance station. There is a beach area and swimming (with lifeguard protection at designated times) is permitted. Fort McRee was also located on the Key, but has been destroyed by time, tide, and weather.

Santa Rosa Island has three separate sections – the Fort Pickens area, the Santa Rosa area, and the Okaloosa area. The Fort Pickens area is named for the Fort built in the first half of the nineteenth century as defense for the Pensacola Bay Navy Yard. There is the remains of a military battery, Battery 233, built on the foundations of two previous batteries, Slemmer and Center. As with Fort Massachusetts, there is a wonderful self-guided tour, through which one can experience history. On this tour, one can learn of the time when Geronimo and his band of Apaches were incarcerated there. Eventually the wives and families of the men joined them.

The Santa Rosa Area and the Okaloosa Area have many amenities: hiking trails, swimming areas, picnic areas, and at Santa Rosa, a ranger station. Fishing is also permitted in designated areas. Most of the Florida areas have visitor and use fees, but they are covered by National Park Permits.

In addition to the islands, there are three major areas of the park on the mainland. One, in Mississippi, is Davis Bayou. There is a visitors' center, a camping area, and picnic areas. All camping sites can accommodate either tents or RVs. There are both hiking and bicycle trails, as well as fishing areas. The visitors' center has many educational activities for all ages. In addition to the educational films, there are many ranger programs designed with the family or special age groups in mind. These are open to the public and very seldom require pre-registration, so if you see something on the website or in any local advertising, call to make sure there have been no changes. Even if there are no special activities listed, the park is a delightful area to simply go and spend the day out-of-doors.

In Florida, the Fort Barrancas area is on the site of a fort built to protect the Gulf Coast from foreign invasion. Much of the fort is intact. A self-guided tour will open the imagination to the lives of those who lived and worked there in a very different time. It is thanks to places like this one and the people who inhabited them that the Gulf Coast is the interesting and safe place that it is today.

The other land-based area in Florida is the Naval Live Oaks Area. This area has one of the most interesting histories of any part of the Gulf Islands Seashore. It was originally a tree farm planted to provide wood with which to build United States Navy ships. It was the first tree farm in the United States. Now it is a national park with a visitor center and park headquarters located here. It has a picnic area and provisions for group camping. It also has several nature trails of varying lengths.

If you are in the Gulf Coast area, and are inclined to participate in outdoor activities, (and if you are on the Gulf Coast, you must be so inclined) one of your very best choices would be some of the activities available through Gulf Islands National Seashore.

Gulf Islands National Seashore:
Ship Islands Excursions: http://www.msshipisland.com
Gulf Islands National Seashore: http://www.nps.gov/guis
Twitter: @gulfislandnps
Directions: Mississippi: 3500 Park Road, Ocean Springs, MS
Florida: I-10 to I-110 at Pensacola. Take Hwy 98 then 399 to the beach. Go West at Fort Pickens Road.

Bellingrath Gardens and Home
Coca-Cola, Camellias, and China Doll Heads

Karen B. Kurtz – Fairhope, AL

Dozens of historic estates flourish along the Gulf Coast, but only one contains an old collection of china and bisque doll heads. Renowned as the charm spot of the Deep South, the beauty of Bellingrath Gardens and Home lies in its antique furniture, rare porcelains, and spectacular year round gardens.

Ever since touring the estate, Bessie Bellingrath simmered along in my mind. While rounding a corner in her home, I was startled to see a group of ordinary china and bisque doll heads, neatly arranged on glass shelves in a locked cabinet. It seemed so unexpected: doll heads near rare porcelain figures from Jacob Petit, Meissen, Jean Gille, and Sevres. Our tour guide casually dismissed them as "those old heads" and moved on, but I continued to reflect on Bessie Bellingrath's collecting habits. Still intrigued months later, I returned to the estate to learn more.

Coca-Cola

Walter Bellingrath moved to Mobile, Alabama, in 1903 to bottle Coca-Cola. Doggedly working a sales territory about 100 miles long, Walter fulfilled deliveries to pharmacies and shopkeepers with hand-operated machinery and a mule-driven cart. Through hard work, perseverance, and innovative marketing ideas, the 35-year old bachelor became a rising star in the Atlanta-based soft drink enterprise.

On a swift trajectory, Walter married his secretary, Bessie Mae Morse, and bought her a spacious home in one of Mobile's elegant neighborhoods. Bessie worked tirelessly to make her home and garden a showplace. Her love for beauty, coupled with a generous spirit, played a major part in their lives' work. For many years, the house at 60 South Ann Street (now demolished) was a highlight of Mobile's famous Azalea Trail.

World War I brought sugar rationing and a limited supply of Coke syrup for Walter's business. When an influenza scare sent him to the doctor; Walter told his physician a fishing camp he'd long admired was up for sale, a former plantation in the 1700s. His physician, knowing Walter's thriftiness, advised him to buy it and "learn how to play." And so Walter did.

Bellecamp

The rustic fishing camp sat on a bluff overlooking the Fowl River, just thirty minutes from Mobile. Fallen trees and debris littered the land, remnants from the 1916 hurricane. Within two years, Walter and his father-in-law cleared the land, renovated old cabins, built a lodge, and proclaimed "Bellecamp" ready for guests.

Bessie transplanted azaleas from their overcrowded Mobilian garden into the woods around the rustic lodge. She discovered Bellecamp's sandy soil and shade was ideal for growing their favorite azaleas and camellias. Today, venerable camellia plants in scores of varieties border most of the walkways.

Bessie's enthusiasm overflowed to Walter and they traveled to see the great garden estates of Europe. When they returned, they hired George Rogers, Mobile's leading architect, to help them create their own floral paradise. Within a few years, ordinary Bellecamp became Bellingrath Gardens, the extraordinary.

Bellingrath Garden

Rogers' vision gave the estate an established, historic look, but he faced a formidable task. He drilled for artesian wells and got a steady flow of undrinkable water due to high sulfur content and its rotten-egg odor. Roger engineered an extensive series of fountains and runnels to transport the water down to the Fowl River. Bessie designed and personally supervised the construction of The Rockery, which leads down to Mirror Lake. Rogers spanned Mirror

Lake with a bridge and populated it with swans, Canadian geese, and other birds.

Rogers replaced an old Satsuma orchard in the adjoining farm with turf, creating The Great Lawn. Today it is luxuriously verdant. Multi-colored annuals, replanted every season, anchor the perimeter.

Rogers and Bessie contacted nurseries and individuals across the Deep South, searching for centuries-old shrubs to fill the gardens. Bessie often paid hundreds of dollars for a single shrub if she thought someone was needy. Walter's Coca-Cola delivery trucks, as well as trains, transported them to Bellecamp. Gardens grew in size; surrounding woodlands were landscaped and planted.

So many people clamored to see the gardens in springtime that Walter and Bessie decided to share them with the public. Invitations went out to national garden club members and local residents; the response was overwhelming. About 5,000 people jammed the roadways! Police officers came out to untangle all the confusion. Walter and Bessie, astounded by the response, decided to open Bellingrath Gardens to the public, establishing a 50-cent admission fee. In 1934, Bellingrath Gardens opened year round.

Bellingrath Home

Rogers finished the 10,500 square foot English Renaissance mansion in 1935. Walter and Bessie moved right in. Rogers used handmade brick and wrought-iron lacework, circa 1800s, on the exterior. Flagstone terraces and courtyard, slate roof and figural copper downspouts, balconies and covered galleries gave the mansion a Gulf Coast flair. Today, the Bellingrath Home is one of few house museums in the world to feature the complete furnishings of its original occupants. Nothing was added, little removed.

Inside, large airy rooms with oversized windows provide kaleidoscopic views of the gardens. Intricate plaster molding decorates every room like frosting. Antique furniture ranges in style from the simple curves of the American and French Empire periods to finely carved acanthus leaves of the Federal period. Porcelain complements the furniture, ranging from the Meissen and Chelsea periods of the 1700s to Royal Doulton pieces from the first half of the twentieth century.

Holidays were a time of celebration for Walter and Bessie. An elegant Chippendale banquet table and chairs (once owned by Sir

Thomas Lipton, creator of the famous Lipton tea brand) fills the Main Dining Room. A Christmas dinner with Uncle Bell and Bessie was an annual treat for their nieces and nephews, who filled the house with laughter and chatter.

For intimate gatherings, guests dined in the Sunday Night Supper Room or Summer Porch. Bessie used Haviland china, a highly desirable Limoges porcelain, in the supper room. The porch has expansive arched windows, tranquil river views, and commanding portraits of Generals George Washington, Robert E. Lee, and Stonewall Jackson.

Walter and Bessie loved to entertain. Silver, crystal, and china overflow in the Butler's Pantry. In the kitchen, a table made from Alabama marble sits stolidly alongside countertops made of German silver, an alloy made of copper, nickel, and zinc, so named for its silvery appearance.

Upstairs, Walter's bedroom features a Jacobean-style desk with mother-of-pearl inlay and a carved four-poster bed. Beyond, Bessie's pink bedroom contains a massive bed attributed to Prudent Mallard, circa 1860. Walter and Bessie didn't have any children. Their nephew and his wife liked to stay in The Purple Room, one of three guest suites in the mansion.

The Purple Room features a mahogany poster bed with elaborate carving, circa 1843. A 1920s Duncan Phyfe sofa adds comfort. In the 1950s, a Memphis decorator suggested refitting a closet with glass shelves to display sixty-six doll heads.

Bessie, who collected fine porcelain, but not dolls, often sat all day in an auction gallery, waiting for her coveted treasure to come up on the block. The doll heads were thrown in with another box lot, where they kept company with other odds and ends in Bessie's basement, until rescued by the decorator.

Molded from bisque (bright, white unglazed ceramic) or china (glazed ceramic), the doll heads are hard-paste porcelain, just like Bessie's rare porcelain figures. Various German doll companies such as Kestner; Alt, Beck, & Gottschalck; and Hertwig manufactured doll heads by the millions before World War I in the Thuringian region. Today, advanced doll collectors consider Bessie's doll heads easy to find though relatively few have survived. Whether ordinary or rare, beautiful old dolls from any period reflect a simpler time, a time when the world moved slower.

Bessie spent nearly forty years amassing antique furniture, rare porcelains, fine china, silver, and crystal to fill her home. She bought treasures in antique shops along the Gulf Coast. She bought from fine shops and major auction houses in New York, Philadelphia, Chicago, and Europe. In addition, people on hard times brought antiques to her.

Delchamps Gallery

The Bellingrath estate stewards a collection of Boehm porcelain sculptures in the Delchamps Gallery. A self-taught American artist, Edward Boehm's knowledge about animals grew from his work as a farm manager and veterinarian's assistant.

Ivory-billed woodpeckers form the focal point of the gallery. Personally presented to Bellingrath Gardens and Home by Boehm and his wife, Helen, legend says the woodpeckers are the largest hard-paste porcelain sculpture ever made. Boehm created the piece for a special London exhibition; it took five months to complete.

Delchamps Gallery honors the late Delchamps family, widely known along the Gulf Coast as founders of a supermarket chain. Boehm's artistry from all periods is illustrated in the gallery, ranging from early glazed works (thoroughbreds, dogs, and mallard ducks) to later unglazed, decorated porcelain like cardinals, bluebirds, and ring-necked pheasants. Bellingrath Gardens and Home manages one of the largest collections of Boehm porcelain in the world.

Bellingrath-Morse Foundation

After Bessie died in 1943, Walter continued to live at home. "The Gardens were Bessie's dream," he said, "and I want to live to see that dream come true." He dedicated the rest of his life to this cause.

Walter died in 1955. He was buried beside Bessie in Magnolia Cemetery in Mobile. The Bellingrath Home opened to the public in 1956. It is listed on the National Register of Historic Places.

Walter left most of his estate, including his business interests, to the Bellingrath-Morse Foundation, a nonprofit trust he established before death for the continued operation of Bellingrath Gardens and Home. The Board of Trustees continues to manage and maintain the sixty-five-acre estate.

With thousands of camellias, azaleas, roses, cascading chrysanthemums, and the famous light show in December, Bellingrath Gardens and Home has truly lived up to Bessie and Walter's dreams: ever-enchanting beauty, constantly changing, and never the same.

Thanks go to Tom McGehee, the curator at Bellingrath Gardens and Home; Scotty Kirkland, former archivist at University of South Alabama; and friend Jo Strycker, who cheerfully loaned her books.

Bellingrath Gardens:
Website: http://www.bellingrath.org
Directions: I-10 to Exit 15-A, Road 16, Hwy 59, South 11 miles to Bellingrath Gardens Road.

Round Island Lighthouse, Pascagoula

Brenda Brown Finnegan – Ocean Springs, MS

Round Island, in the Mississippi Sound, was named by French explorer Pierre LeMoyne d'Iberville in 1699, "on account of its form," although it seems to have always been a curved island according to many old maps. It lies approximately three miles south of Pascagoula, Mississippi.

In the 1800s, the Mississippi Gulf Coast had numerous grand hotels, resorts and health spas which served people from New Orleans to Mobile. Long piers extended into the Sound to off-load passengers and freight. Lighthouses were deemed necessary to protect ships from the shoals in the Mississippi Sound, so necessary that in 1825 a federal law stipulated the death penalty for those caught burning a building on lighthouse property.

On May 18, 1833, Congress granted $7,000 to Marshall Lincoln of Boston, Massachusetts for construction of the first lighthouse on Round Island. Construction was completed on December 1, 1833, at a cost of $5,895 for the forty-five-foot brick tower. The eleven lamps hung forty-eight feet above sea level and were visible for up to fourteen miles. The first keeper, Curtis Lewis, apparently lived in quarters built prior to the lighthouse's completion. Several of the subsequent keepers are documented by David L. Cipra in his book,

Lighthouse, Lightships and the Gulf of Mexico.

Round Island became an important historical landmark when unarmed mercenaries gathered there on August 7, 1849, for an intended mission to free Cuba from Spain after the Polk administration's offer to purchase Cuba from Spain for $100,000,000 was refused. On August 11, President Zachary Taylor declared the proposed invasion was in violation of American neutrality laws. Taylor was quite familiar with the Pascagoula area, having enjoyed a brief family vacation there the previous summer at the McRae Hotel, prior to his election as president. He took action to prevent the mercenaries from leaving the island by having the United States Navy ships, U.S.S. Albany and two other warships, blockade Round Island on August 28, an event subsequently refered to as "The Round Island Filibustering Affair."

The Lighthouse Keeper at the time, Samuel Childress, was apparently ignorant of the naval orders when he loaded his supplies in Pascagoula and headed for Round Island. Armed sailors intercepted his schooner and took Childress and his two sons prisoner. After producing a copy of his official appointment as lighthouse keeper, they were released. The mercenaries, however, did considerable damage to Round Island Light Station before they dispersed. There were two deaths from the incident; one man was stabbed and another died of "brain fever."

"In the end," according to Charles Sullivan, in his book, *Mississippi Gulf Coast, Portrait of a People,* " both sides backed down." The blockade was lifted on September 5, 1849.

In 1852, the Federal Light House Board took over responsibility for administering lighthouses. There were twelve lighthouse districts, three of which were in the Gulf: the Seventh, Eighth and Ninth. Round Island fell in the Eighth Light House (or Naval) District. Louis (or Lewis) Henry Fisher of Pennsylvania was appointed keeper as of November 15, 1853, with an annual salary of $500.00. A fifth order Fresnel lens was temporarily placed in the old tower that year.

Capt. Danville (or Daniel) Leadbetter, Corps of Engineers, Inspector 8th District, noted that the first lighthouse had deteriorated markedly by 1855, and recommended that a new tower and dwelling be combined. Leadbetter proposed a tall brick tower bulging outward at the bottom to enclose an octagonal keeper's dwelling raised on iron screwpile stilts. The Light Board approved a more conventional conical tower. Records do not show what happened to the first Round Island lighthouse.

According to Mary E. Hogue's unpublished collection in *Pascagoula, Round Island Lighthouse, General History* (found in the Pascagoula Library's veritcal files), $8,000 was appropriated for a new lighthouse on August 18, 1856, but it was not completed until 1859, at a cost of $7,130.97. The new fifty-foot red-brick tower was constructed 500 feet to the northwest, and a fourth order Fresnel lens was installed. The remainder of the appropriation was transferred to Jupiter Inlet Light Station in Florida.

Three significant hurricanes hit the Gulf Coast the following year. The first on August 15, 1860 did considerable damage. During a second storm, on September 15, the keeper, Louis (or Lewis) Henry Fisher, his wife and six children, took refuge in the tower for thirty-six hours, without food or water. Everything they owned was lost and every building on the island, except for the tower itself, was destroyed.

During the Civil War (1861-1865), Round Island served as a terminal for cotton smuggled down the Pascagoula River. On January 5, 1865, Union forces from Ship Island captured a quantity of cotton and tar there where the Confederates had hidden it.

The lighthouse lens was removed by the Confederates to Montgomery for protection and to keep Union forces from navigating in the Mississippi Sound. At the U. S. Navy's request, the lens was returned and the light was relit on March 10, 1865, by James Duggan.

A gale on April 30, 1867, damaged the keeper's dwelling and kitchen (separate structures in those days) and when repairs were perfomed in 1868 the lighthouse deck was expanded, adding a ring to watertight the lantern room, as leakage had been a problem since construction. The corbels, shown in later photographs, gave the upper section a trumpet shape.

Over the next few years the lighthouse served various purposes. Some of the light keepers farmed in their spare time to supplement their salaries, as the local newspaper noted June 4, 1880, "First watermelon of the season was brought to this office last Mon. by

Mr. H. C. Anderson of Round Island." Round Island was used as a quarantine and inspection station for yellow fever in the late 1800s. Officials housed on the island were responsible for fumigating inbound ships. A resolution of the Jackson county Board of Health on Wednesday, September 8, 1897, appointed Dr. B. F. Duke the quarantine physician at Round Island. Dr. W. R. Kell, local health officer, was requested to procure the necessary funds and equipment from the State Board of Health.

Widows were occassionally appointed as keepers, and their daughters thereafter, as family members were often unofficial, unpaid assistants to the keepers, helping with the day-to-day work of the lighthouse upkeep. Mrs. Margaret Anderson of Bombay, India (probably light keeper Charles Anderson's widow), was listed as keeper at Round Island from 1872-1881, at an annual salary of $625.00. Upon her death on January 31, 1881, Mary Anderson, probably her daughter, served one year as acting keeper.

In the book, *Instructions to Light-Keepers*, July, 1881, there were instructions on every aspect of a keeper's life, including the use of the "Funck Mineral-Oil Float Lamp," with diagrams of both the lamp and Brown's Steam Fog Signal included. Fog signal instructions were included as well as recipes for whitewash and purifying rainwater that may have been contaminated with chloride of lead from run-off on the roofs. The use of powdered chalk or whitening was recommended. Tables of keepers salaries were listed as well as "Allowance of Provisions" of pork, beef, flour, rice, raisins, ship biscuit, brown sugar, tea, coffee, butter, beans or "pease," vinegar, molasses, pickles, potatoes, and onions.

According to records provided by his great niece, Katie E. Steen of Pascagoula, Epps Danley was sworn in at Round Island on March 10, 1902, (as assistant) serving there until 1905, when he was transferred to the Pascagoula River Station.

On September 27, 1906, a hurricane ravaged the island and Keeper Hansen reported losing his board fences, cistern, workhouse, water closets, and chickenhouse, though the lighthouse stood. He reported that breakers crashing against the lighthouse reached halfway to the top. That same storm gutted the East Pascagoula River lighthouse and destroyed the Horn Island lighthouse. The body of the keeper at Horn Island, Polish-born Charles Johnsson, was found in the wreckage the next day. His wife, Catherine, and eighteen-year-old daughter, Marie, were never found.

On July 1, 1939, the Bureau of Lighthouses was consolidated with the United States Coast Guard, which assumed responsibility of all U.S. Lighthouses. Round Island Lighthouse was automated in 1944, but was discontinued as an official aid to navigation in 1946. It continued as a day beacon until 1954, the same year the keeper's home burned and the assistant keeper's house was sold.

By the 1980s the abandoned tower had suffered greatly. The open door allowed vandals to deface bricks and destroy the contents, and erosion allowed water to surge inside during storms. The City of Pascagoula assumed ownership of the lighthouse and forty-eight acres of Round Island in 1986. It was registered with the National Registry of Historic Places in1988.

In 1998, shortly after The Round Island Lighthouse Preservation Society was organized, Hurricane Georges toppled the lighthouse into the Gulf on September 27. The ventilation ball, lightning rod, and bricks were recovered by workers and dedicated volunteers. Efforts to stabilize it in 1999 were undermined by Hurricane Katrina on August 29, 2005. Private and governmental efforts resulted in moving it ashore in July 2010.

It was rebuilt within sight of the Pascagoula River, on an island of grass near the Highway 90 Bridge entering Pascagoula. The company that recast the lantern gallery is owned by one of 1920 Keeper Arnold Steiner's relatives, Ken Steiner, and brick salvaged from the collapse in 1998 was used to rebuild the structure, now with a new steel core. Steiner said about 65 percent of the 6,000 pound lantern gallery is original. The restoration took about a year to complete and was delivered to the site on July 09, 2012. A topping ceremony was held in May 2013, replacing the newly rebuilt lantern gallery to the top of the lighthouse, and the structure is being bricked with very similar brick to the original.

When complete, it will be the highlight of a new Lighthouse Park, linking downtown to the site.

Works Cited:

Mississippi Gulf Coast, Portrait of a People, Charles Sullivan
Lighthouse, Lightships and the Gulf of Mexico, David L. Cipra
Pascagoula, Round Island Lighthouse, General History Mary Houge
Record of Light-House, Light-Vessel and Fog Signals, Keepers' Names; National Archives
Dimitry Lighthouse Log: (Made available by Rene Gautier Hague of Pascagoula.)
Instructions to Light-Keepers, July, 1881 (This book was provided by Renee Gautier Hague of Pascagoula.)
The Mississippi Gulf Coast, Portrait of a People, Sullivan & Powell
The Sun Herald, Biloxi, MS
The Mississippi Press Register, Pascagoula, MS

Round Island Lighthouse
Location: Pascagoula, MS
Website: http://www.roundislandlighthouse.org
Contact: Jen Dearman, Grants Administrator
City of Pascagoula, 630 Delmas Avenue,
Pascagoula, MS 39568
Phone: 228-938-6639
Email: jdearman@cityofpascagoula.com

Pascagoula River Audubon Center

Eco-tourism on the last free flowing river in the lower 48 states

Philip L. Levin, MD – Long Beach, MS

The Pascagoula River Audubon Center (PRAC) in Moss Point serves as an outspoken advocate of preserving our local ecosystems. With special devotion to the Pascagoula River basin, it provides conservation information through bird watching programs, bayou-boat guided tours, and school field trips. A branch of the Mississippi Coast Audubon Society, the PRAC's goal is to prove eco-tourism can make saving the wetlands profitable for business, the residents, and the environment.

Pulling into the PRAC's camp, one feels the peace brought on by the love of nature. A double row of freshly painted birdhouses dry in one corner. Mourning doves attack a line of plastic and wood birdfeeders. A boat stands at the dock ready to bring visitors out on a nature exploring adventure. A passel of schoolchildren talks excitedly, just back from a nature walk. PRAC is housed in an old white home converted into use as a center, a nature scene from the seventies, bringing the visitor into a world of unspoiled natural beauty.

"With a new five-thousand-square-foot building slated for opening next year, the Center is focused foremost on bird and wildlife conservation," Mark LaSalle, Director of the Center told me. "We are part of the National Audubon Society (NAS). Established in 1905, NAS is the second oldest continuously operated conservation society in the world; only the Sierra Club is older." Named after John J. Audubon whose fame is based on his drawings of birds in the wild, the Audubon society has a national, state, and local presence.

Mr. LaSalle explains the Center has three target audiences: nature tourists, local residents, and school children. Nature tourists come from across the planet to experience the unique natural bayou atmosphere with special guided boat tours. These trips, led by homey naturalist Benny McCoy, take participants on a two-hour plus tour along the idyllic channels of the Pascagoula River and its associated bayous, an opportunity to find scurrying fiddler crabs, alligators sunning on fallen logs, and thick black grasshoppers gathered by the dozens. We trolled right under three nests of juvenile ospreys. Members of the eagle family, the ospreys look much like a bald eagle, though a bit smaller and whiter. On the trip I took, travelers from Germany snapped innumerable photos from the seats behind me, while next to me a family from Missouri told me they come to the Mississippi Gulf Coast every year to enjoy our pristine beauty. This trip is a must for any visitor to this region. Call (228) 475-0825 to make reservations for their boat trips, running twice a day on Tuesdays, Thursdays, and Saturdays, $25 for adults, $15 for children, with a senior discount available. Each boat holds twenty tourists.

The Center's second targets are local residents, with whom the Audubon Society works to demonstrate the value of protecting the watershed's integrity. "We deal with local developers through the wetland laws, showing land owners and local officials the economic potential of ecotourism." Mr. LaSalle reports this has become easier since the hurricane demonstrated the dangers of developing in flood zones. "This area has incredible biodiversity. Relatively speaking, it's in great shape." Local volunteers often act as stewards by adopting certain birding sites; they will visit their chosen site often, clean out trash and accumulated debris, and work on restoration by uprooting invasive species, such as popcorn trees.

The third branch of the Audubon's mission is school children. The program offers summer camps, and, during the school year, full day field trips. Forty children will attend each day, half going out on the boat in the morning while the other half participates in nature walks and other building activities, switching roles in the afternoon after lunch. Though education stands as an important part of their mission, Mr. LaSalle says, "You don't develop a business plan based on school buses."

PRAC's main partner is Mississippi Coast Audubon Society, through the Audubon's national office in New York. The satellite state office in Mississippi resides in Holly Springs, as far north as you can go and still be in the state. "Audubon is here to promote and protect, in this area, by promoting nature tourism with over 100,000 of acres preserved for natural habitats," Mr. LaSalle reports.

PRAC works in the lower six counties in Mississippi, though is focused on the Pascagoula River Basin, the last large, fully free-flowing river in the lower forty-eight states. No major dams or water control structures exist anywhere on the eighty-two miles of the Pascagoula River, nor the much longer two rivers that join at Merrill to form the Pascagoula, the Chickasawhay River and the Leaf River. From the mouth to the outlet, PRAC is involved. "All the money we raise supports our work here," Mr. LaSalle said.

One of their big projects is being responsible for putting up the signs and designating the area, with the Harrison County Sand Beach Department, for protection of the least tern colonies, including the tiny white tepees designed to act as chick shelters. Usually the county Sand Beach Department cleans the beach by plowing under all the trash. This disturbs all the natural beach growth, taking away habitats for the birds' nesting. PRAC erects fences around designated nesting areas, and with the County, putting a moratorium on cleaning those areas, the plants grow for the birds' use. The tepee chick shelters PRAC provides give the chicks protection from the numerous natural predators. One of the biggest colonies is near Beauvoir, and other areas are chosen based on how the natural beach access dictates where crowds tend to gather. Once the areas are designated for protection, another native bird, the Black Skimmer, come to nest in colonies. The Skimmers nest almost exclusively in the Gulf. The Least Terns nest from the Northern Gulf to Florida. Least Terns nest in early April, Black Skimmers in the latter part of June, with their colonies adjacent.

Of four hundred and twenty bird species found in the state of Mississippi, 389 of them are found in habitat maintained by the Mississippi Coast Audubon Society, with 327 species of birds found on the Pascagoula River. The rest are shore birds, a major component to the list. Shore birds are best seen here in the winter; even arctic birds come winter here. Some of the more common species are the Common Loon and the American White Pelican, which breeds in Michigan. The Bonaparte Gull comes down here during the winter months.

Mr. LaSalle designates four groups of birds that can be seen by birdwatchers:

1. Resident birds found year round, such as mockingbirds, cardinals, bluebirds, and mourning doves.
2. Migrant birds that fly through twice a year, though don't stay. Typically these are the warblers that winter in South America, and do a spring migration and don't breed here. Dauphin Island is famous for their sightings. These include the Hooded, the Black and White, the Canadian, and the Kentucky warblers. Some seasons have a flurry of unusual sightings, such as a colony of Rosebreasted Grosbeaks. Migratory birds will return in the fall.
3. Breeding birds winter in South America, and in the spring come here to breed. An example would be the Prothonotary Warbler with its characteristic bright yellow head. These birds love to nest in cavities in trees or sometimes in an old shoe. Other examples of breeding birds are the Hummingbirds, Purple Martins, and the Least Terns.
4. Overwinter birds are those who breed in the northern US and Canada, and come here for the winter. Some of these are the Common Loon, American White Pelican, Marbled Godwit, Rudy Turnstone, and the Sanderling, a small white sandpiper often seen darting in and out of the waves on the beach.

Besides birds, the area is an excellent spot to see many other kinds of wildlife, such as the Yellow Blotched Sawback Turtle, which is exclusive to the Pascagoula River. Actually, seventeen different species of turtles live on this river, with several endangered. A common animal not endangered is the wild hog, a perpetual pest with a tendency to eat away the roots that keep the riverbank intact. The types here descend from the Russian Boar and the Barrel Hogs, the latter imported from Europe, reaching weights of five hundred pounds. For those in the mood for hunting, there's no limit on wild hogs – and they make good eating!

These bayous are prominent nursery grounds for seafood, especially shrimp and crabs. Fishermen will delight in the multitude of native river species, including both fresh and saltwater flounder, flathead, tabby fish, and catfish. "You'll never know what you're going to get until you reel them in," Benny McCoy said. "Every time you come out here, you'll see something different."

An immense variety of plants add another spectrum for nature lovers, vibrant with a collage of colors most prominent in the spring and fall. Sawgrass, Black Needlerush, and bullrash with their sharp edges can cut the careless. The Black Needlegrass gets rid of its salt by pushing it into one stem, which then dies and is sloughed off. The Bulltongue Airhead's leafs belong to the Duck Potato family with edible starchy roots as big as your thumb. It's believed it's from this plant that the Pascagoula Tribe and River obtained their name, for the word "pascagoula" means "Bread making" in Choctaw. Trees of several species are present, with Black Gums the most common tree in the swamp. By the way, the difference between a marsh and a swamp is the swamp has trees, so there's less brackish water. Other trees commonly found in the area are the Tupelo Gum, the Dwarf Palmetto, and the Bald Cypress. Like most cypress, the Bald has big buttes, with muscles on their base. Indians would use the palmettos for shingles on their roofs.

Established by the late Judy Toups, the Mississippi Coast Audubon Society dates to 1975, much of its direction due to her devotion. Following the Audubon Society's special interest in birds, Mrs. Toups established a Mississippi coastal birding trail map, still in use today. She was a prolific writer of nature articles, particularly with the American Birding Society and articles promoting bird watching and conservation. Another of her projects, working with the county governments to specify protected breeding areas for the Least Tern and Black Skimmer, was so successful, in early 2008 a section of U.S. Highway 90 in Gulfport bordering the nesting areas she sought to protect was renamed the Judith Toups Least Tern Highway.

Mark LaSalle, the current director, was trained as a biologist, with his degree in fishing biology. An educator all his life, he considers himself a wetland ecologist, specializing in tideland marshes. For a time he worked with the Army Corp of Engineers, and then for the State of Mississippi. With the Mississippi State Extension Service, out of Starkville, he developed a Master Naturalist program that trains teachers in wetland society, and creates naturalist volunteers.

Pascagoula River Audubon Center
Website: http://pascagoulariver.audubon.org
Address: 7001 Frank Griffin Road in Moss Point.
Phone: (228) 475-0825

Good Karma Café of Gulfport and Ocean Springs Gives Visitors a Taste of the Exotic

Cecily Cummings – Gulfport, MS

Every traveler loves to find that hidden gem in the city he or she visits, a place where the locals go for great food at great prices. If you're traveling down Pass Road in Gulfport or on Government Street in Ocean Springs, chances are you wouldn't look twice at the "hole in the wall" restaurants known as Good Karma Café and Good Karma Medley, respectively. The Café shares a space with a check-cashing store, while Medley is next door to an old-fashioned gas station. Despite their nondescript exteriors, locals know the food served inside is delicious. If you passed them, you'd miss very remarkable jewels!

When you think of Gulf Coast cuisine, oysters, shrimp scampi, and crawfish come to mind. Every casino has a massive buffet and there seems to be a catfish restaurant on every corner. If you're looking for something different, a taste of the exotic perhaps, this is the place for you. The Good Karma restaurants serve the best and most authentic East Indian cuisine you can find outside of India.

Their dishes are one-hundred percent vegetarian and vegan friendly. If you're a meat and potatoes kind of person, don't be deterred. The food is so tasty you'll never think to ask, "Where's the beef?"

"Most of our customers aren't vegetarian," said Beverly Cobb, manager of Good Karma Medley. "They just love the food."

The health conscious individual should know that all the restaurant's foods are organically grown on the owners' farm, and are free of genetically modified organisms. All ingredients are plant-based and contain unrefined ingredients.

Head cook Maharani Berg said healthy eating "makes people feel good. You can eliminate a lot of illnesses by eating right."

Good Karma is owned and operated by the people of the New Talavan Community in Carriere, MS. The residents are members of the International Society for Krishna Consciousness, also known as the Hare Krishna religion.

As their website (www.newtalavana.org) explains, New Talavan is a 1200-acre, thirty-year-old spiritual community practicing sustainable organic agriculture and dairy farming. They are progressing toward agricultural and economic self-sufficiency. Their goal in opening the Good Karma restaurants is to create a healthier community by educating its customers to educate themselves on what they eat.

For those who are interested, the restaurant provides information about the pros of a vegetarian diet and the cons of a heavy red meat diet. According to restaurant reading material, a vegetarian diet lowers the risk of diseases like obesity, heart disease, high blood pressure, diabetes, and colon cancer.

When you arrive, you are greeted warmly by the staff. Newcomers are told about the restaurant and their offerings. You never have to worry about knowing what to order at Good Karma. Each day, head cook Maharani Berg serves only one set menu with a variety of items. If you still feel hesitant about the food, ask for a free sample before ordering.

You will be served a salad with a house-made dressing. Next, you will be brought an Indian soup, such as split yellow dahl with kale. The main course consists of items such as mixed vegetable rice, cabbage subjii, mango tomatoes, chutney, samosas and spiced tea. For dessert, "Yogi oats," better known as oatmeal cookies, are served. On some occasions, Burfi (the Indian version of cheesecake), spiced cookies, and Russian teacakes are available. Berg also uses healthy spices such as cardamom and turmeric, which are good for the mind and body. Never heard of most of the foods? Don't worry – you're in for a surprise and a treat.

"The regulars will say, 'I don't know what I'm eating and I don't care because it's so good,'" Cobb said.

Berg, Cobb, and staff will always answer questions and tell you the names of the dishes you are eating and what's in them. After a few visits, words like "paneer," "subji," and "upma" become integrated into your vocabulary.

Many customers are amazed by the variety of items available each week with primarily vegetables and grains on the menu.

"I think I have more variety in my diet now since I don't eat meat," said Cobb.

Though the food may be exotic, the manners are close to home. In the tradition of Southern hospitality, Berg almost always offers you a second helping at no additional cost. Tips are not accepted, as Good Karma is staffed by volunteers, though donations may be made to the "cow fund" at their farm. Make sure to arrive early before supplies run out. Leftovers, if there are any, are given to the Gulf Coast Rescue Mission.

The staff takes the time to get to know customers, and Berg will often sit with customers and talk. She offers them gifts from the shop on holidays and invitations to important events at New Talavan. Their most popular festival is the regular Hare Krishna Love Feast every Sunday.

"It's not about the money," Berg often says of her business. "It's about making people feel good." She treats her customers like family and teaches the importance of eating healthy for the good of body and spirit.

After eating, you can browse through the gift shop that offers an array of unique Eastern clothing, including shawls, saris, and men's shirts. Jewelry, incense, essential oils, natural soaps and much more are also offered. You can also shop her display of natural grocery items to try your hand at Eastern cooking at home. Aside from exotic dry goods and spices, she offers locally made honey and hand-blended herbal teas.

Available at both branches are natural sweets made by Cobb. Delicious items include strawberry whole-wheat tarts, vanilla almond cake, and Mexican chocolate cake, among many others. It doesn't get any better than her natural sea salt fudge. While in town, check and see if you can register for one of Berg's cooking classes; offered occasionally, they fill very quickly.

Almost every season Good Karma offers a special party with food, music, and dancing. Her family members have started the Bhakti Caravan, a musical mantra group. They play at the temple events and even at weddings and other occasions.

Good Karma has survived and thrived on word of mouth alone. They have not advertised on TV, the radio, or in magazines. "We have our regulars," said Cobb, "but it's amazing how we get new people every week."

A restaurant regular once described Berg as an "artist of the kitchen." She doesn't follow a recipe, and she throws in a dash of this and that by instinct. "I cook differently," Berg said. "I don't follow the rules."

Cooking has been in her family for generations. "I was born in Malaysia, and I learned to cook from my mother and sister," she said. "Our neighbor owned a café, where I learned to cook rice and vegetables and season with curries."

When her spiritual group decided to come to the United States, they asked her to come along to teach cooking. She worked at the group's restaurant called Govindas in New Orleans, LA, for eight months before marrying her husband, John Berg, and moving to New Talavan in 1974. She cooked for her family and the people on the farm, but never considered herself "a fancy cook."

A friend from Long Beach often visited the temple and urged her to open a restaurant. Berg began cooking for the masses after Hurricane Katrina in 2005. All the residents of New Talavan survived the catastrophic natural disaster, and they rallied to help the community.

Good Karma is an affiliate of Global Food For Life, which is in keeping with the ancient Vedic culture of practicing good hospitality. It is now the world's largest vegetarian/vegan food relief program, with representatives in many parts of the world, according to their website (http://www.ffl-gulfcoast.org).

If you would like to learn more about Indian culture, the International Society for Krishna Consciousness, or agricultural sustainability, visit the source: the New Talavan Farm in Carriere.

"We encourage customers to go. We're surprised at how many show up," Cobb said. "It's family friendly, with no drugs or drinking." New Talavan was built thirty years ago under the guidance of their spiritual master Srila Prabhupada. Their motto is "simple living and high thinking."

According to their website, New Talavan takes its name from one of the twelve forests in the region of the Indian city Vrndavana, a place Krishna was said to have lived 5,000 years ago. It was a place of rest and relaxation for Krishna and His cowherd friends.

The farm came from humble beginnings, consisting of a handful of worshippers from the New Orleans temple who came and started planting a garden. Not long after, these devotees relocated to Talavan. They worked together for many years to make it the successful temple and farm it is today.

New Talavan has been protecting cows for over thirty years. Across India, the cow is venerated for supplying humankind with essential and nutritious food. Indians refer to cows as the "mother and father of humanity." They believe in a reciprocal relationship between humans and cows, with humans caring for the animal and the cow providing food for its master.

According to their website, the most important aspect of New Talavana is its spiritual life, including their temple and their deities. The deities are given offerings five times a day and are dressed and worshiped at specific times according to Vedic scripture. Guests are invited to attend the worship services, especially during scheduled *darshan* times for the weekly Sunday Feast at noon. Arrive early to get a parking space since services begin punctually.

The restaurants have reading material about the Hare Krishna religion and its practices, though the beliefs are never forced on customers. The information often clears up false preconceived ideas and stereotypes of the religion.

"It lets people see what it is and what it isn't," Cobb said.

New Talavan accepts applications for organic gardeners and farming volunteers. Guests may work in their three-acre garden or assist the resident gardener with planning the next season's crops and improvements.

"We have so much support," said Cobb. "Whenever we need help, someone comes to help."

Volunteers are allowed to camp on a spot of their choice on property. Showers, restrooms and vegetarian food are supplied. Participation in temple services is not required, though you would be asked to respect their spiritual principles while on the property, as their website explains.

The next endeavor of New Talavan is to open a restaurant in

New Orleans, LA. Berg's son, Goshi, also a great cook, will open a café with Michele Baker, the founder of Swan River Yoga in New Orleans. Theirs will be the one of the few completely vegetarian/vegan friendly restaurants in the city. Their menu will include items such as curd burgers, vegan wraps, an Indian buffet, a fresh juice bar, fresh smoothies, vegan baked goods and chai tea, according to their website.

As more volunteers become available, Cobb said they would like to move Good Karma to a larger location and expand their hours. She would also like to help the homeless and the poor by starting a voucher program for meals.

Good Karma has prospered, thanks to its delicious food and strong relationships the staff has built with the community. "I love my job because the customers are like friends," said Cobb. "We're happy to be here."

"They're very supportive," said Berg of her customers. "They're always thankful for what we do. I never thought we'd find such generous customers."

Good Karma restaurants are for those who crave something new, whether it is food or an awakening. Above all, getting to know the staff and its customers builds awareness about achieving physical and spiritual wellbeing.

"The type of people we meet here are looking for something different, something higher," Cobb said. "We've built a huge community of friends on the same path."

"I sleep well knowing I've helped and done something good for the day," Berg said.

Good Karma Medley is located at 522 Washington Avenue,
Ocean Springs, MS 39564
Good Karma Café is located at 412C Pass Road,
Gulfport, MS 39507
Hours: Tues-Sat 11:30 am - 2:30 pm (or until food sells out)
Contact: (228) 575-9102
https://www.facebook.com/maharani.berg
http://www.ffl-gulfcoast.org, http://www.newtalavana.org

Mary Mahoney's Old French House

If Walls Could Talk

Kara Martinez Bachman – Mandeville, LA

Walking into Mary Mahoney's Old French House is like walking into the past. Steeped in the ambience of various decades that have played out within its aged walls, this Biloxi landmark dishes up not only renowned food, but also a heaping dose of the old world. Really, though, Mary Mahoney's is not about a certain date or about a certain era—it is about the comings and goings of time.

Throughout the years, the historic-home-turned-restaurant had been a residence to many. Claims by restaurant staff include the legend that Jean-Baptiste Le Moyne de Bienville, Governor of the Louisiana Territory and a prime figure in the history of the South, once lived there. More recently, just before it became Mary Mahoney's in 1964, two little old ladies lived there. The building has had many owners and many lives.

Although there is some disagreement on record about the exact date the home was built—some guess it wasn›t until the early 19th century—the Mahoney family believes they know the exact date.

"The house was built in 1737, so it's one of the oldest structures in America. It's pretty much an icon of the Gulf Coast," says Eileen Mahoney Ezell, daughter of founder Mary Mahoney's and one of the restaurant's current owners. "This had been the home of Bienville – that's why it's known as the Old French House. A lot of people say, 'Are you a French restaurant?' We say, 'No, it's *always* been known as the French House.'"

The past seems to echo from walls that have witnessed generations of families, and raging winds and water from occasional hurricanes, and milestones that give meaning to the lives of many on the coast. Mary Mahoney's is not simply a restaurant; it's a time capsule.

"If these walls could talk!" Ezell says. "The people that come through have come here as children, some of them have had rehearsal dinners here, gotten married here, or come back as grandparents with their grandchildren. We've been here so long that families have grown up with us."

The minute you step into the walled courtyard area of the restaurant complex, it is clear that you are in a place that has witnessed many scars and many joys. The restaurant displays menus and other ephemera that document its forty-eight years as a fine dining establishment and its deep history as a home. On display throughout are mementoes related to the property's history and to the history of Biloxi, including "water line" signs denoting heights that flood waters reached during Hurricane Camille's 1969 flood and Katrina's deluge in 2005.

The old world of this building seems so different from the modern ones of its immediate surroundings. Just across Beach Blvd. from the hulking properties of the Beau Rivage and Hard Rock casinos, the Old French House may be dwarfed in size, but it remains a solitary giant in local culture. Having survived through generations, the brick and stucco building has withstood the test of time in ways that few others have.

A meal served under the high ceilings and chandeliers can feel like a trip to decades past. Alternatively, a sunny lunch on the front porch, with its wall of windows, is an absolute delight. Live oaks provide the view just outside, which is no doubt similar to that enjoyed by residents of old. The oaks were probably the same, only back then they had seen a wee bit less and had heard slightly fewer gulf winds blow onshore.

Dining on the porch feels like a step back to a time in the second half of the twentieth century. Mature waiters in elegant jackets and bowties fill water glasses and dexterously remove silver domes from serving plates; the whole affair feels a little like some sort of throwback. It feels like those times before the restaurant business grew dominated by Olive Garden and Outback Steakhouse and the type of standardized restaurants that are not at all about stability, or family, or the allure of *real* local cuisine.

The "family" feel of the restaurant is enhanced by the longevity of the wait staff. "When they work here they just don't leave," says Ezell. "It's a family run business and we treat them like family. I have a couple of waiters who have been here over forty years—I think three of them."

The Southern coastal vibe is not just for locals. Tourists, some of them notable, flock to the restaurant despite a burgeoning collection of fine dining options offered by local casinos. From politicians to media personalities, Mary Mahoney's is a hotspot for immersing in the best of the south.

"We send John Grisham a care package every Christmas because we're in two of his books, *Runaway Jury* and *The Partner*," Ezell says. "And he calls our gumbo world-famous, so he gets a nice care package every Christmas. He says it's his favorite restaurant in Mississippi, that it's always their Christmas dinner, or Christmas Eve dinner. He loves gumbo."

The writer is not alone among high profile people who delight in the landmark restaurant's seafood-heavy menu offerings.

"When Denzel Washington was here, he ordered like ten gallons [of gumbo] to ship to his North Hollywood home. He did a cast party. A lot of people have tried it and they love it."

There is much talk in all quarters about this favorite dish.

"One of our waiter's grandfathers was one of our first cooks. He did the gumbo and we've been making it the same ever since… we have consistency. If people ate the gumbo ten years ago, they're gonna come back and be like, '*This* is what I *remember*.'"

A family affair since it opened, sometimes people will return after many years to find little has changed, aside from a minor menu tweak or two. The real changes are not concrete and visible—they consist primarily of new memories, of new snapshots to hang on someone's wall.

News personality Anderson Cooper can count himself among those who contribute to the history of this stolid place. Ezell tells of Cooper's visit as a child. No doubt, the Mahoneys remembered him because he was the young son of heiress Gloria Vanderbilt and screenwriter Wyatt Cooper. The journalist had forgotten this earlier Biloxi visit until his return after Katrina. He came back to cover the aftermath of the storm and chose the restaurant as a meeting point for a CNN interview with John Grisham.

"When Anderson came here after the storm," says Ezell, "My brother [Bobby Mahoney] told him, 'Welcome back.' And he [Anderson] said, 'What are you talking about?' And Bobby said, 'You and your brother were about ten years old, and you came with your daddy—he was here for a book signing.' And it was like stars went off…he said 'I remember going to a water park!' And Bobby said, 'Yep, you came in wrapped in a towel.'"

Sometimes it seems that comings and goings of notables and the exemplary ambience of the restaurant overshadow the food; however, both are worthy of acclaim. From a delicious light lunch of shrimp salad to a rich dinner of buttery seafood, Mary Mahoney's is a seafood lover's dream.

"When people come in here and say 'I'm allergic to seafood' it's like, 'Well, you're probably in the wrong place!'" laughs Ezell, who grew up with the restaurant and who, like most raised on the coast, loves seafood.

Although there are a few chicken dishes for lunch, such as Fried Chicken Breast Almondine and a nice collection of beef offerings for dinner, including Filet Mignon and Prime Rib, the name of the game at Mary Mahoney's has always been seafood.

The most popular menu items, the "World Famous Seafood Gumbo" and favorites such as the fried softshell crabs, draw the most attention. However, Mary Mahoney's offers a wide variety of savory seafood choices that reflect a coastal vibe of freshness and abundance. Much of the menu is not for calorie-counters or for culinary lightweights; this kitchen means business.

One example is the Flounder Imperial, a more recent addition to the nightly menu. This stuffed fish offers an indulgence that goes above and beyond. "We de-bone the flounder and we stuff it; not with a crabmeat dressing, but with *solid* crabmeat." At $44, it is one of the pricier menu items—but Ezell reports that diners really enjoy the over-the-top seafood indulgence. From fried shrimp and fried oysters to lobster tails, there is a nice variety to choose from. All dinner entrees start at $25, and lunch entrees start at $12.95. There is also a nice wine list and enjoyable selection of appetizers. (Prices listed valid summer 2013).

Dinner at Mary Mahoney's would not be complete without a serving of bread pudding. This southern favorite is served with a buttery rum sauce; it is the perfect way to round out any meal.

Although the food is delicious, there is something special about *just being there*. There's something relaxing about enjoying the beautiful setting. There's something meaningful about dining among residual memories of wedding banquets past, or of legends French leaders who shaped the Gulf Coast, or of family meals served by a favorite black-tied waiter.

Thankfully, Mary Mahoney's understands that what they have on their hands goes well beyond mere sustenance.

"We ship the gumbo all over the country," said Ezell. "I had one guy who said, 'I was in there and I had your gumbo, and when I got it at home it really didn't taste the same.' I said, 'Sir, I can't ship atmosphere.' And he said, '*You're probably right.*'"

This article originally appeared in *Legends* Magazine.

Mary Mahoney's Old French House Restaurant
110 Rue Magnolia, Biloxi, MS 39530
Phone: (228) 374-0163
Website: http://www.marymahoneys.com
Hours: Mon-Sat, 11 am - 10 pm

The Old Biloxi Cemetery

John Cuevas – Atlanta, GA
Photographs by Jason Taylor

Overlooking the Gulf, only a shell's throw from the hustle and bustle of Beach Boulevard is the Old Biloxi Cemetery (1166 Irish Hill Drive). With moss draped oaks sprinkled among a myriad of headstones and mausoleums now covered with the greenish-brown patina of a bygone age, this historic site is a welcomed contrast to the flashing neon lights of the twenty-four-hour casinos just minutes away.

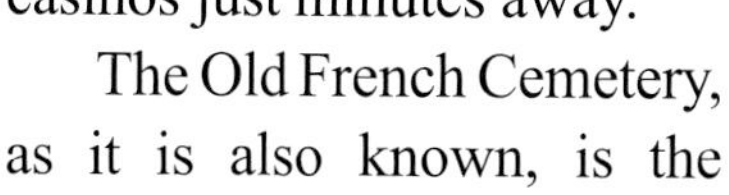

The Old French Cemetery, as it is also known, is the resting place of many of the earliest pioneers of the Mississippi Gulf Coast. While wandering through the marble monuments and simple graves, one can almost feel the drama of these peoples' lives whispered in the breezes blowing gently from the Gulf. Some of their stories are well known, while many others are lost in the forgotten past.

The land was situated near the proposed site of Fort Louis, the intended capitol of the Louisiana territory, and had been used for burials since the French colonized the area in 1700. Other groups of people living nearby also used the land for burial, although it did not become the official cemetery of Biloxi until the heirs of the property owner, Louis Fayard, donated the land to the city in 1844, shortly after his death. Louis Lalanzette Fayard (1758-Bef 1844) settled on the coast in 1793, becoming a well-known and respected member of the community. He and his wife are both buried in the cemetery.

Although plans to build Fort Louis were abandoned when the French governing council voted to move the capitol back to New Orleans, the land continued to be an important burial site. Historians believe the cemetery was also used for a series of mass burials. There were at least two occasions when large numbers of interments occurred. The first was the result of the John Law fiasco, known commonly as the Mississippi Bubble. John Law (1671-1729) had taken control of the Louisiana territory by a royal grant in 1717, with the purpose of making the new colony profitable. To entice settlement on the coast, Law created deceptive brochures and promotional materials presenting the territory as a Garden of Eden. Even with his slick marketing, very few Europeans volunteered to move to the coast. Those who willingly chose to come were offered free land, provisions, and transportation to the new territory. Instead of the paradise they were promised, the people faced starvation, disease, and virtually no development. As a result, many hundreds, and maybe thousands, died.

The yellow fever scourge that began in Louisiana in 1796 also caused the death of many along the coast. By the end of the sixty-seven-year epidemic, approximately one out of every twelve persons had died from yellow fever in New Orleans alone. The names of those who succumbed to the disease are lost forever, since there were no burial records before 1841. Adding to the difficulty of identifying the dead is the lack of surviving headstones. The earliest markers were made of wood and other impermanent materials, since there were no appropriate stones native to the coast. These crude markers eventually deteriorated, having been ravaged by storms, vandalism, and the effects of time, leaving the identities a mystery for the ages. The oldest identified grave in the Biloxi cemetery is that of Michel Batet, a native of France who died in May 1811 at the age of 34.

Watery graves have always been a problem in the low-lying areas of the coast. It was not uncommon for a coffin to fill with water and actually float out of its hole. In an attempt to prevent this dramatic event, heavy stones were placed in the caskets with holes drilled in the bottom and top to allow the water to flow through. Unfortunately, these efforts often failed to solve the problem.

As a solution, Spanish Governor, Estéban Miró (1744-1795) in New Orleans pressed the city officials to adopt the wall vault system that was popular in Spain at the time. Spain had devised an economical method of above ground burial. This method worked perfectly for the wetlands of the coast. The practice of burial in vaults quickly became popular, particularly among the wealthier families who could afford larger and more ornate tombs. The cemeteries that incorporated this method, including the Old Biloxi Cemetery, were strikingly different from the graveyards commonly found in other parts of the country, whose green lawns, shady trees, and marble headstones were nothing like the tombs in Louisiana and Biloxi.

One of the first vaults in the Old Biloxi cemetery that incorporated the Spanish method was that of Juan de Cuevas (1762-1849), famous in local history as "The Hero of Cat Island." Cuevas, who owned Cat Island by way of a Spanish land grant, reportedly fired the first shots against the invading British during the Battle of New Orleans. When he died in 1849 his body was first buried on the island, but later moved to his newly constructed vault in the Old Biloxi Cemetery. Four years later when his wife, Marie, died she was also buried in his tomb.

The Spanish system allowed for multiple burials in the same vault. The tombs were never opened before a year and a day had passed allowing time for the first body to naturally decompose. The extreme temperatures within the vault aided this process. When the door to the tomb was opened again, all that was left of the body inside amounted to little more than bones. The remains were then swept into a hole at the back of the crypt called a *caveau*, and the newly deceased was then slid into the vault in the original position where the first body had been. With this method, it was not uncommon, regardless of the vault's size, to be used many times for the burial of several generations of the same family. Each new name was then chiseled in the marble door alongside the older names.

One of the most dramatic examples of multiple burials in the Old Biloxi Cemetery is the eight-foot high Reynoir family vault located near the entrance. It was built of Georgia Marble in 1896 for Frederick "Arthur" Reynoir (1832-1897), a successful land speculator. When Hurricane Katrina toppled many of the tombs and headstones in 2005, the marble door to the Reynoir vault was torn loose. It revealed a list of names and burial dates engraved on both sides. There were so many that the door had been reversed and eleven new names were added to the front. The last member of the Reynoir family was interred there in 1965.

Among those buried in the Old Biloxi Cemetery are heroes and villains, rich men and poor, but mostly are found ordinary people whose names reflect the heritage of most of the area's residents. Many deserve recognition, but there are far too many to list.

To name a few, one of the quirkiest and possibly most talented persons buried there is the now famous George Edgar Ohr, Jr. (1857-1918), the self styled "Mad Potter" of Biloxi. Ohr's talent blossomed after he began to produce art pottery. His technical skill is unmatched today. Possessing a playful spirit and a gifted flair for self-promotion, he fostered the idea that he was crazy. Beneath his eccentric façade was a genius in the art of pottery. The new Ohr-O'Keefe Museum at 386 Beach Blvd., Biloxi, was created to display and promote his exceptional works.

Another colorful individual buried there is John R. Guilhot (Jean Guillot) (1877-1959), "The Hermit of Deer Island." Guilhot, a native of France, was originally a businessman in Biloxi. When his home burned down, his wife reportedly left him and took the insurance money. He then moved out to Deer Island where he preferred to live as a hermit. A crude shack was his home for 37 years until his death in 1959. When tour boat captain Louis Gorenflo brought his passengers by Deer Island, Guilhot would row out to meet the boat and serenade the tourists with French folk songs.

One of the national figures in the cemetery is James Park Caldwell (1841-1912). Caldwell was only fourteen when he, along with four other students at the University of Miami, founded the Signa Chi fraternity. He graduated from Miami at the young age of sixteen and went on to study law, eventually ending up in Biloxi where he practiced law until his death. He was the only one of the founders of Sigma Chi who fought with the Confederacy in the Civil War.

Anthony Nicolas Benachi (1858-1916) was the son of cotton broker Nicholas Marino Benachi (1812-1886). Anthony's father was born on the Greek island of Khios. His uncle Emmanuel was the mayor of Athens. Benachi moved with his family from New

Orleans into their summer home in Biloxi around 1900. His father, Nicholas, introduced the first Greek Orthodox Church in this country in New Orleans. Today there are 540 parishes in the Greek Orthodox Archdiocese of America.

Raymond "Medeaux" Caillavet (1838-1898) was a former Biloxi Mayor (1877-1882). He served in several positions in city government, but was most useful as an interpreter of legal documents for wealthy Creoles from New Orleans, as well as his fellow citizens. He was fluent in both French and English, and was one of the only settlers who could read and write.

William K. M. Dukate (1853-1916) was one of the fathers of the coast seafood industry during the period when Biloxi was recognized as the "Seafood Capitol of the World." Along with his partners, Lazaro Lopez, William Elmer, William Gorenflo and James Maycock, they brought to the coast the successful canning techniques they had learned in Baltimore.

Edward Joseph Younghans (1858-1934) was a prolific photographer of important sites and buildings all along the coast. Many of his photos appeared on popular postcards during the "golden age of the postcard" (1907-1915), preserving for future generations the historic images of buildings long destroyed.

Buried among the wealthy and influential people is Pleasant Reed (1854-1936), a former slave and member of the largest African-American family in Biloxi. Although he was of modest means and could not read or write, he managed to live well through his hard work and determination. He built a sturdy home for his family during the 1800s. Over time he continued to upgrade the house and its furnishings, giving it the appearance of a much finer home. Reed's house was donated to the Ohr-O'Keefe Museum.

A visit to the Old Biloxi Cemetery at 1166 Irish Hill Drive can captivate your interest for an hour or for an entire day. You will find it to be a pleasant way to relax and get to see the final resting place of some of the men and women who laid the foundation for today's Mississippi Gulf Coast.

Old Biloxi Cemetery
1166 Irish Hill Drive
Biloxi, MS
Phone: (228) 435-6279

The Dusti Bongé Art Foundation is an Art Destination in Biloxi's Rue Magnolia

Cecily Cummings – Gulfport, MS

Highway 90 in Biloxi is lined with numerous casinos, chain restaurants, and heavy traffic. If you're looking for a quiet retreat and a chance to experience the best of Biloxi, take a detour on Reynoir Street and visit the historic Rue Magnolia.

This locale is in the heart of Biloxi's downtown area and features many personally owned and operated businesses along a quiet walkway. The shady promenade is lined with magnificent live oaks where one can hear the sounds of birdsong above the background traffic traveling Highway 90. It's the perfect place to spend a quiet afternoon while in the middle of a bustling Biloxi downtown.

You can stop on a park bench and feed the pigeons or grab a café au lait and beignets at Le Café Beignet. Rue Magnolia is home to salons, a vintage clothing store and many art galleries including Prima Donna Consignment, the Artist's Cooperative, and Gallery 782, among many others. The Ohr-O'Keefe Museum is also in close proximity. All afford excellent opportunities to view and buy local art.

Of course, no visit to Biloxi (or the South, for that matter) would be complete without dining at the nationally renowned Mary Mahoney's. The historic Old French House has served presidents, celebrities, tourists and locals alike. Request a table on the glassed-in porch, where you have a view of the garden, fountain, and resident artist Carmen Lugo working in her Strange Bird Studio directly across the street.

If you are not able to visit Rue Magnolia during the daytime, try to catch a "Finally Friday" event that takes place the first Friday of every month from 5-8 pm. The businesses stay open late and live music is often featured. Guests have the chance to win a gift card to some of the area businesses.

One art destination that mustn't be missed is the Dusti Bongé Art Foundation located at 132 Rue Magnolia. The organization was founded in 1995 to promote the works of Biloxi's amazingly talented Abstract Expressionist painter. The Foundation is housed in what is known in the area as "The Creole Cottage," a quaint little building with old-fashioned charm. The building was Biloxi's first library. Visit the Cottage and you will come to know the life and works of a fiery Southern woman who rubbed elbows with the likes of ground-breaking artists such as Willem de Kooning and Jasper Johns in New York in the 1920s.

In 1995, a group of Bongé devotees established the Foundation. They formed a board of directors for what would become a nonprofit organization honoring and promoting Bongé's work.

"We want to make sure she is not forgotten," said Olivia Simon, Foundation registrar. "We want to tell her story and promote arts in the community."

Simon said they are currently working on computerizing Bongé's catalogue of artwork, so that her works may be presented to galleries and museums throughout America. "A huge priority is preservation and conservation," said Simon, as Bongé painted in a time before archival materials were widely available.

The Foundation offers changing exhibits of works from the Bongé Collection, the Bongé family members and friends of the artist. They offer occasional art workshops and educational information about Bongé. While visiting the Foundation, a staff member can tell you about the enigmatic Dusti Bongé while you view her incredible artwork.

Bongé was born Eunice Lyle Swetman in 1903 in a large turn-of-the-century home in Biloxi. She earned her nickname "Dusti" from her childhood habit of playing outside and getting her dresses covered in dirt. Her grandson, Paul Bongé, said that even as an adult, she was never afraid of getting dirty and wore old overalls while painting in her studio. Paul described Dusti as having a slight

Southern accent, fiery strawberry red hair, and piercing pale blue eyes. Simon described her as being "eccentric and ahead of her time."

As a young woman, she wished to pursue a career as an actress. She attended Blue Mountain College, a Baptist school for women in north Mississippi, and then moved to Chicago to study drama at the Lyceum Arts Conservatory in the early 1920s. She joined several theater traveling road companies in Chicago, Illinois. It was during this time she met her future husband, Arch Bongé, a 6' 7" Nebraska native who was a painter. From 1926 to 1928, she lived in New York and acted in films produced in Long Island, at the same time performing in vaudeville, drama, and musical comedies. Arch began working as a theater doorman and in film production by Astoria Studios in Long Island to support his artistic endeavors.

Their courtship made headlines in a New York newspaper in a story entitled "Handsome Theater Doorman Wins a Beautiful Heiress." The story recounted how the two met and fell in love, but many aspects of the story were greatly exaggerated. Dusti was the daughter of a banker, but was by no means an heiress.

Under Arch's influence, Dusti experimented with painting during their first years of marriage. Her most memorable early piece came as a result of an argument between the two. Dusti painted Arch a picture as an apology, leaving it in his studio. He was so impressed with her painting that he encouraged her to work with him. She agreed so that the two could spend time together, but came to love painting on her own.

Soon after the birth of their son, Lyle, the Bongés realized they were tired of big-city living. They headed back home to the South in 1935. There was not much of an art scene on the Coast at the time, though she did share the Coast with future talents George Ohr and Walter Anderson. However, in Biloxi, Archie had more time to paint and encouraged Dusti to do the same. Not long after coming home, Arch passed away from Lou Gehrig's disease. Archie's studio became a place of consolation, and she began to paint more seriously.

Dusti always said, "If you're cursed with being an artist, you have to find a way to make a living." She admitted that art was "a completely useless and totally selfish endeavor." To support herself and Lyle, she took a government job collecting rent from shrimp pickers, images of which inspired some of her early paintings.

Throughout the 1930s and '40s, she depicted many nature scenes around Biloxi, including the woods and walking trails along the Tuxachanie River. The South Mississippi beaches inspired her love of color and a fascination with shape and perspective. These first works owe much to Arch's influence.

She took her work to New York to exhibit in the 1940s and found success at the Betty Parsons Gallery. She was the first woman to ever have a solo exhibit there. "To be invited to be part of a gallery stable of famous artists, barely three years after beginning to paint, is remarkable for any artist," critic Daniel Haberman remarked in 1982.

The Betty Parsons Gallery played a key role in the emerging American art scene of the 1940s and 1950s by promoting the likes of Mark Rothko, Hans Hofman, and Clyfford Still, all forces behind the New York School of Abstract Expressionism. It was said Willem de Kooning never missed a Bongé exhibit at Betty Parsons. Mark Rothko would become good friends with Dusti and even visit her and his godson Lyle in Biloxi.

As reported by The New York Times in 1956, "An interesting New York debut is made at the Betty Parsons Gallery by Dusti Bongé, a non-objective painter from Biloxi, Mississippi (who) devises sternly colored compositions … some of which are of considerable authority and inventiveness." Betty Parsons tried to persuade Dusti to move back to New York, but Dusti refused. She had stillness and space at home in Biloxi.

"Working alone in Biloxi, Mississippi, Bongé ([whose] 'talent is developed in solitude,' said Goethe) has managed to create a truly moving and different body of paintings," Haberman said.

Modernism suited Bongé's intellectual perceptions and her natural bent towards color and intuitive self-expression. Her style changed from realism to abstraction, and "dreams formed a bridge between the two." Dusti created some notable works in the Surrealist style from 1945 to 1955, most notably, the "Keyhole People," the last works in which the subject matter was clearly identifiable. This series, painted in neutrals and oranges, features abstract human-like creatures with large keyholes in their bodies.

Dusti felt Cubism and Surrealism were too structured; this structure limited how much she could say and how much emotion she could express. The emerging style of Abstract Expressionism was more liberating for Dusti as it emphasized the unconscious. It was free of judgment, ego, and labels. It took no effort to explore the emotions. With this new style, she joined the ranks of Pollock, Rothko, and De Kooning. Though inspired by other Abstract Expressionists, she was never imitative or derivative. Dusti went on to try color field abstractions late in life, and even experimented by painting with a broom straw and a limp, wet string dipped into ink. She created small pieces on "Joss" paper, a thin paper burned to make offerings to the dead in Asian cultures.

She insisted on changing her style every five to ten years to keep her work new and fresh. Once a style was mastered, she thought, it was "too easy." One's work must change or the artist is trapped. Dusti also warned other artists to "never start believing in your own publicity," otherwise you won't grow as an artist.

Dusti Bongé, Dream Series #4, oil on canvas. 1962 (28" x 18")
Used by permission of the Dusti Bongé Art Foundation
Photographer: Billy Dugger

Bongé did not have a favorite painting among her works and worked hard for each to be up to her personal standard. Paul recalled once seeing smoke billowing from a pile of burning canvases outside her studio. "I'll not have unworthy, substandard work existing," she explained. Many she might dislike because she used the canvas to experiment with a new technique that did not quite work out.

Dusti saw a lot of changes in her lifetime. She was born before women had the right to vote and in an era of segregation. She had no problem expressing her opinion on hot ticket items. She also supported the women's rights movement, feeling that women should have equality in the work world and be free to live life as they chose. In her final years, she never lost her zest for life. She loved traveling to exotic locales and spending time with her friends and family.

Lyle once asked her what she thought about death. She responded, "I never thought about it, but I'll let you know if anything occurs to me." Life was immediate and she did not feel inclined to speculate about anything beyond that immediacy.

Bongé died in 1993 at the age of 90, leaving behind around 250 oil paintings and thousands of works on paper. "Dusti is one of the few people I have known, through 70 years of living, who was an artist in everything she did. She simply looked at the world and her surroundings through an artist's eyes," said Nancy Terrell, editor of Bongé's autobiography, Dusti Bongé: The Life of an Artist.

Bongé was never worried about being famous. She knew she was regarded as an important figure in the Abstract Expressionist movement, but thought it was "no big deal" and felt recognition was unnecessary. Though Dusti is not as well known as her Abstract Expressionists counterparts, her work is her legacy. Her paintings, like their creator, are "open, free, unburdened, full of possibility, energized" (eulogy, 1993). She had her own way of doing and seeing things, and her paintings are evidence of this unique vision. The story of her life is evident in every brushstroke of her artwork. With one look at her paintings, the viewer will feel the passion and intensity she invested in her work, her family, and her life.

Visit the Rue Magnolia and stop by the Dusti Bongé Art Foundation to learn of the life and art of a gifted woman. It is located at 132 Rue Magnolia, Biloxi, MS 39530-4217. Hours are Mon-Fri, 10 am to 4 pm, or by appointment. Call 228-432-7660 or consult the Internet at http://www.dustibonge.org.

Dusti Bongé Museum
132 Rue Magnolia, Biloxi, MS 39530-4217
Hours are Mon-Fri, 10 am to 4 pm, or by appointment.
228-432-7660
http://www.dustibonge.org

Sie's Place, "Where nice people come to have a nice time"

Elaine McDermott – Gulfport, MS

On the corner of Division and Reynoir Streets in Biloxi, cradled between IP and Beau Rivage Casinos, stands the past home of "Sie's Place." Now closed for almost forty years, this historic landmark will forever harbor the spirit of Sie Simon, the soul of the Biloxi music scene of the 1950s.

Lured to the Gulf Coast by its seafood industry, an influx of immigrants migrated to Biloxi in the 1880s. Included in the migration was a large Slavic population originating in Dalmatia, the coastal region of Croatia. They earned their living harvesting oysters, trawling for shrimp, and working in seafood factories. Many of them settled in Point Cadet, known as "The Point" in east Biloxi, a peninsula wrapped around by Back Bay to the east and north and the Sound to the south. In the 1900s Slavonian Lodge and the fisherman's church, St. Michael's, were built. Because they lived, worked, prayed, and played on The Point, it became the cultural center for the immigrants.

Sie Simon's parents, Joe and Catherine Simon, arrived from Lebanon in 1904 with four dollars, raising Sie and his eight siblings on Fayard Street in a small home and a warm, fun-loving family circle. Though Sie was an avid fisherman, this personable, fun-loving entrepreneur decided to turn his passion for music and love of people into a profitable enterprise.

In 1934 the main strip in Biloxi, Highway 90, was lined with hotels, souvenir shops, seafood restaurants, nightclubs and strip clubs. Illegal gambling flourished, and illegal liquor flowed freely. It was in this milieu Sie opened his country/western club.

Sie's Place was an immediate success, becoming known throughout the South as the premiere country/western club. In its heyday, Sie's hosted many performers of the Grand Ole Opry and the Louisiana Hayride, including Elvis Presley, Minnie Pearl, Ernest Tubbs, Marty Robbins, Hank Snow, Faron Young, Webb Pierce, Ray Price, Jerry Lee Lewis, the Everly Brothers, and the most famous of the country/western stars, Hank Williams, Sr.

For forty years top Nashville acts entertained there; beer and whiskey flowed, and nickels clanged in the slot machines as cherries, plums, and lemons rolled across the screen. No matter where on the Coast an entertainer performed, he would end up at Sie's unannounced and climb up on the bandstand. Entertainers loved performing at Sie's; it was like a homecoming, and Sie treated them as family. Patrons enjoyed a special night out whenever crowd pleasers Minnie Pearl, Elvis, or Hank Williams appeared. Minnie Pearl would come on stage wearing her signature hat with the price tag hanging down and shout, "How-dee, I'm just so proud to be here!" Sie's Place was a springboard for Elvis Presley, helping to launch his career.

Gerrie Weldon, Sie's daughter, quotes her father as saying of Sie's, "Where nice people come to have a nice time. If they weren't nice, we'd boot them out on the sidewalk." Gerrie describes a childhood that probably made her and her sister, Kay, the envy of their friends. "Kay and I were raised to the beat of the "Sie Simon Shuffle" (written by Pee Wee Maddux) because our bedroom was dead set against the bandstand. We often shared our table with Hank and Audrey Williams. People asked us how we felt to have Hank Williams in our home. Well, we thought he went to everyone's home."

Gerrie remembers, "We made bottle dolls from long neck Jax beer bottles and dodged people on our skates going in and out of the nightclub." In spite of the long hours Sie spent running a business, the girls were never neglected. "We always sat to eat as a family, and at that dinner table we bonded," states Gerrie. "Daddy's girls were very important to him and we knew it."

Sie Simon was a man of the people; he had personality and charm that drew people to him. Gerrie thinks of him this way, "A smile and a handshake, coming from a man in a suit and a tie, generated warmth and friendship to any person he met."

Sie Simon often recruited his acts from neighboring nightclubs. After the performers made their scheduled appearances, Sie would invite them to Sie's Place, "Come down, see what you like." In the fifties and sixties, one of the famous clubs on Highway 90 was Gus Stevens' Restaurant and Lounge where many aspiring stars got their start. Some of the notable among the entertainers were Andy Griffith, Jerry Van Dyke, and Dave Gardner. It was not unusual for a performer to end his last show at Gus Stevens' and wind up the night on Sie's stage. On a side note, Gus Stevens' nightclub was dealt a fatal blow in 1967 when Jayne Mansfield, her attorney, and the driver of the car were killed on their way to New Orleans after Mansfield's last show.

Hank Williams and Sie became great friends. Sie was a father figure who was there for Hank in good times and bad. He would take him deep-sea fishing, and always had the kitchen table stacked with boiled shrimp when Hank was in town. One time when Hank was at the Buena Vista Hotel, he asked Sie to come listen to a song that he had just written. Sie told Hank he didn't think a song about Cajun food would have universal appeal. Later that song, "Jambalaya," held the number one spot on U. S. Country Charts for fourteen weeks.

Sie's daughter, Kay, told of how one day a taxi driver knocked on Sie's door and told him he was there to collect for a fare from Nashville. Sie asked the driver how much the fare cost. It was $1,000.00. Sie exclaimed, "$1,000.00, who's out there?" He walked outside to find Hank sitting in the taxi.

On January 1, 1953, at the age of 29, Hank Williams died of a heart attack in West Virginia while being driven to Canton, Ohio, for a New Year's Day appearance. Sie Simon was an honorary pallbearer. In Hank Williams' childhood home, now a museum, hangs a picture of Sie and Hank. The last public performance before Hank's death was only a few weeks earlier on December 7, 1952, at Sie's Place.

In 1974 Sie closed his nightclub and retired. Although he missed mingling with the crowd, moving from table to table with a handshake and a smile, Sie enjoyed the time spent with his family and the time spent fishing in his boat. For several years after Sie's Place closed, Nell Hebert, a forty-year employee, organized an annual Reunion Ball with proceeds going to the Biloxi Boys Club. Kay recalls that many of the old timers from Sie's would hobble in on canes or walkers, throwing away these supports when the music started to "kick it up on the dance floor."

When Kay was a young widow with a small child, she met Alton Bankston. On their first date, they went to her father's club, Sie's Place. A few years after Sie's closed, Alton opened Bankston's Paint in the building, replacing beer cans with paint cans. The paint store was a huge success for thirty-nine years, and many a Coast home is covered in Benjamin Moore paint. When Hurricane Katrina came roaring down on the Coast, the paint store was flooded with seven feet of water. Hanging near the entrance, the collection of photographs of entertainers who had performed at Sie's was severely damaged. Some were salvaged, but water stained.

Katrina was not the first hurricane to strike the building. Kay remembers the hurricane of 1947 (hurricanes were not given names then). "Gerrie and I were bundled up in blankets and carried to Sie's Place, and we slept on blackjack tables." Gerrie says it was all great fun because they could drink all the cokes they wanted and play the slot machines. In Hurricane Camille, Sie's sister, Alice, fled from her home in the middle of the night to take refuge upstairs in the club.

Never before had a hurricane as destructive as Katrina hit the Coast. Two years after it struck, the Bankston's Paint business was sold. In 2012, the store was vacated by the new owners, and Kay and Alton decided it was time to sell the building, wanting to find the right owners for this landmark, an indelible part of their family's history and of Biloxi's history. Their search ended when they met with the Board Members of Seashore Methodist, and the property was bought to serve as a Mission to the needy.

Country music no longer reverberates off those walls, but soon joyful music will fill the building. The microphone no longer will be held by country music legends, but by Methodist ministers whose pulpit will stand on the spot that was once a dance floor. The crowds will still come and everyone will be warmly welcomed.

Yvette Mulcahy, an employee of the Biloxi Visitors Center, states that now, forty years after Sie's Place closed, guests still inquire about it. One visitor, after viewing a video on Hank Williams in the Visitors Center, wanted to visit Sie's Place. Learning that it was closed, she asked Yvette for the location of the building. She said she had to see it because her dad had talked so much about the good times he had there.

On July 28 and 29, 2012, a movie about Hank Williams, *The Last Ride*, was presented at the Saenger Theater in Biloxi with over 900 people attending each of the two showings. Dale Greenwell in the D'Iberville Press wrote, "Leaving the Saenger Saturday night, two weeks ago, among many friends and strangers, the mood in the crowd was one of warm remembrance of days gone by, memories that we share of a wonderful period in our lives."

In 1990, when Sie Simon died at the age of 79, Vincent Creel wrote in The Sun Herald, "Sie Simon put Biloxi on the map as a regular stop for dozens of country entertainers, and in most cases he became friends after treating them to fishing trips, boiled shrimp, or seafood dinners."

Sie Simon's death marked the end of an unforgettable era in the city's history. When Sie's Place closed in 1974, that's the day the music died in Biloxi. Today the stage is bare, the song has ended, and the dance floor is deserted. However, nothing can dim the memories of those golden days when Minnie Pearl graced the stage with her folksy humor about Grinder's Switch, a young Elvis Presley brought his blend of country/western and rhythm and blues to Biloxi, and Hank Williams sang to a full house those soulful lyrics that imitated his troubled life.

Location of Sie's Place; 856 Division Street, Biloxi, MS

The Lynn Meadows Discovery Center: Enriching Hearts and Minds

Lauren Clark – Mobile, AL

Nestled in the beachfront community of Gulfport, Mississippi, the Lynn Meadows Discovery Center is an educational treasure for children and parents alike. As the first children's museum in the state, the Discovery Center broke the traditional museum rules by allowing visitors to touch, talk, learn, and enjoy.

The project was first funded in 1991 by the Gulfport Junior Auxiliary, with co-founders Rose Alman and Carole Lynn Meadows leading the team. After extensive renovations to the former Mississippi City Elementary School, the 15,000-square foot Discovery Center opened in May of 1998.

When Hurricane Katrina devastated the Mississippi Gulf Coast in 2005, the Lynn Meadows Discovery Center remained standing, but the storm surge destroyed the entire first floor of exhibitions and office space. The nearby education building, pavilion, and gymnasium were also extensively flood-damaged.

"Hurricane Katrina served as a reminder of how important the Lynn Meadows Discovery Center is to our community and to our children," said Cindy DeFrances, Executive Director of the Lynn Meadows Discovery Center. "Employees couldn't get the doors reopened fast enough. We were able to provide a safe distraction from the utter devastation of our beautiful coastline and become a place that parents could come together to begin the conversation of rebuilding our lives and our community."

After much refurbishment and repair, the Center re-opened on June 6, 2006 with a pavilion featuring three multi-purpose rooms. Later phases of the renovation included the opening of the *WINGS Performing Arts and Education Center* on April 23, 2009.

In the exhibit *It's A Matter of Science*, children touch a tornado, construct building block creations, and play with multi-wheel pulley systems. *The Super Colossal Climbing Sculpture* is a three-story tall ropes "climber" for visitors who are young and young-at-heart, with slides and multiple tiny passageways that entice children to stretch and climb to their limits. *The Mississippi City History Hotel* allows visitors to "check in" and browse through the 1890's style lobby shops. *The Outback Express* is a wooden locomotive and cars that "depart" the Dolan Avenue Depot. Aspiring reporters can investigate local wetlands through *WLMDC-TV*.

In addition to the indoor exhibit space, the Discovery Center offers six acres of outdoor play space where children can check out family movie nights and the spacious and spectacular Tree House Village. Space is also available for art instruction, workshops, and birthday parties.

"Our beautiful grounds are unique to a children's museum," adds DeFrances. "We will be capitalizing on our Gulf-front location with the opening of "Lynn Meadows on the Green" later this year. An acre of land south of the existing property has been purchased and will be used for environmental education, including lessons on native plants and animals and walking trails to encourage outdoor exploration. We look forward to educating the next generation about how important our natural resources are to the future health of the planet."

The nationally-recognized WINGS Performing Arts Program annually involves 500 young people from the first to twelfth grades to explore the performing arts. The program was selected as one of twelve recipients for the nationally prestigious *Coming Up Taller* Award presented by Former First Lady Laura Bush. Several WINGS participants have been chosen to receive Presidential Service Awards. On a state level, WINGS has been recognized with the Mississippi Governor's Award for Excellence in Arts Education and the Mississippi Humanities Educators Award.

During the school year, the *Bear Cub Club* is offered as a daily program for toddlers under five. The Club is designed to stimulate a love of literacy and children's creativity and imagination with stories, music, puppets, and special visitors. *Saturday Surprises* offer unique activities and programs designed to enhance the museum exhibits. Children may fashion a clay pinch pot, enjoy a special WINGS show, dabble with sand painting, create a unique collage using a torn paper, or learn a new painting technique with plate rubbings.

Pam Pannell, a Bear Club member and mother of two children, is an enthusiastic supporter of the Discovery Center's activities. "If you have children or grandchildren, I highly recommend giving them the opportunity to play, learn, and experience all that Lynn Meadows has to offer," says Pannell. "Thank you to the friendly administration and staff and all of those who support Lynn Meadows and make it such a special educational experience for my young children each time we visit."

The Lynn Meadows Discovery Center also offers a plethora of summer camps for students from elementary school through the twelfth grade. The offerings include *American Dream: Cowboys and American Girls*, in which children discover the local history of the Gulf Coast and Mississippi City, *Join Me under the Sea*, which explores water, sea-life, boats, and our very own Gulf Coast, and the always-popular *Princesses and Pirates* Camp. Kids who dig zoo animals and creepy, crawly friends can attend *Lions, Tigers, and Bears...OH MY!* or sail the seven seas and discover new cultures during *Around the World in Five Days*.

WINGS Summer Camps include a *Ten-Minute Play Festival* and a *Crash Course in Comedy*—during which campers will learn to write, perform, edit, and star in comedy sketches. The *Crash Course* camp builds social skills, creative skills, and public speaking expertise. A special performance on the last day of camp will leave family and friends roaring with laughter!

Fans of MGM's *The Wizard of Oz* will want to join the Discovery Center's Musical Theater Camp. Students will study stage movement, voice, choreography, set design and construction, and costume design. A musical production of the classic story of *The Wizard of Oz* will be performed at the end of the session.

Through these activities and more, all designed to simulate the real world of South Mississippi, children visiting the *Lynn Meadows Discovery Center* learn about the past and the present.

The Discovery Center's creators believed that it is with a better understanding of themselves and their community that children can grow to be responsible, global citizens.

The Discovery Center enjoys incredible support from the Gulf Coast community, including countless volunteer hours donated by Mississippi residents. "I have been a volunteer at the Lynn Meadows Discovery Center for two years, and I am proud to be a part of an organization that takes the business of play so seriously," says Margaret Hover. "Our dedicated staff ensure that the museum's mission to inspire children, families, and communities through interactive educational experiences and exploration is met on a daily basis."

Teachers looking for field trip opportunities can contact the Discovery Center to book a group visit. Special group rates are applied to pre-formed groups such as schools, churches, home-schooled groups, or after-school groups. Staff and volunteers will work to make each field trip a unique and memorable experience. Groups may choose areas to visit and amount of time spent on each activity. Picnic areas are available, weather permitting.

The Discovery Center offers a night-out for parents looking to expand their culinary skills and spend a fun evening with friends. On Tuesday nights, Coastal Mississippi chefs fire up the Center's Viking kitchen and share a lively evening of cooking tips and tricks. Throughout 2012, 720 amateur chefs met for the museum's weekly adult cooking classes. Reservations are required.

In 2012 the Discovery Center welcomed 62,000 visitors, hosted group and school field trips serving more than 11,000 teachers and students, and presented ten stage plays that reached more than 30,000 audience members and participants. Three thousand visitors were admitted at no charge on monthly Free Friday Nights. Two new exhibits were introduced in 2012: *Solar Sunflowers*, in partnership with the Department of Marine Resources, and *Chimney Swift Tower*, a project to provide museum visitors with an up-close view of the process of nest building and raising fledglings.

The Lynn Meadows Discovery Center celebrated its fifteenth year of operation in 2013 with a host of new programs and updates, including a $25,000 grant from IP Resort & Casino to update the science room. The Discovery Center also received a $1,000 grant from the Anthony Dartez Endowment Fund to purchase new exhibits for the Disability Room. The current Mexico exhibit will be converted into an Africa exhibit in late 2013, and bi-monthly "Science Saturdays" are planned, in partnership with Mississippi Gulf Coast Community College honors science students.

Many local businesses support the growth of Lynn Meadows Discovery Center, including Drew Allen, President and CEO of Allen Beverages, Inc. "Our company has been involved with the Lynn Meadows Discovery Center since its inception. We first sponsored the grocery store and since have been involved as a Business Buddy for many years," says Allen. "We have watched Lynn Meadows grow its programming and outreach in our Coast community over the years with pride. We urge all businesses on the Mississippi Gulf Coast to get involved with Lynn Meadows. It is money well spent."

The Discovery Center has been named one of *Mississippi Magazine*'s "Top Attractions for Children" in 2010, 2011, and 2012. The Center received a Five-Star rating from Trip Advisor and a "Let's Move" Museum Designation from the Institute of Museum and Library Services.

The Discovery Center is open Tuesday-Saturday from 10:00 a.m. through 5:00 p.m. and on Sundays from noon - 5:00 p.m. Regular museum admission is $8.00 for children and adults. Military personnel and senior citizens are $6.00. Infants under one year of age are free. On weekdays, visitors are treated to special pricing of $3.00 after 3:00 p.m. on Weekdays and $5.00 admission on Sundays.

A year-long membership with the Discovery Center offers families and individuals additional amenities and benefits, which include unlimited free general admission for one year, as well as invitations to exclusive members-only exhibition previews, receptions and special events. Members also enjoy a discount at the Discovery Gift Shop, a discount on birthday parties, facility rentals, and camps, and special ticket prices for events, including *WINGS* productions.

The Lynn Meadows Discovery Center
246 Dolan Avenue, Gulfport, MS 39507
Phone: 228-897-6039
Website: http://www.lmdc.org
Hours: Mon-Sat, 1 am - 5 pm; Sunday, Noon - 5 pm

The Institute for Marine Mammal Studies Center for Marine Education and Research

Valerie Livengood – Carriere, MS
Photos by Abby Livengood Chatelain

Every week we read about the need to improve the education of American citizens. Unfortunately, too many people associate learning with tedious bookwork or boring lectures. What if it were possible to learn about science and nature while having so much fun that it didn't even seem like education? The Institute for Marine Mammal Studies Center for Marine Education and Research in Gulfport (IMMS) has managed to find a way to do just that. Don't let the stuffy academic-sounding name fool you. A visit to the Center for Marine Education and Research is just plain fun!

The Institute for Marine Mammal Studies is a 501(c)(3) non-profit organization established in 1984. Their multiple purposes of public education, conservation, and research of marine mammals and sea turtles in the wild and under human care are fulfilled in numerous ways. They are the leading provider of rescue, rehabilitation, and return to the wild for stranded or injured marine animals in the Louisiana-Mississippi-Alabama region of the Gulf Coast. A state-of-the-art veterinary hospital provides care for sick or injured dolphins and other species. Research facilities and funding are provided for both graduate students and scientists studying a wide range of scientific disciplines. Plus, their Center for Marine Education and Research (CMER) provides on-site educational programs for students and visitors, and is the only facility of its kind in the region. The IMMS does all of this and much more. The CMER provides a place for IMMS to fulfill its mission and share its work with the public.

The first thing you ought to know is that the CMER is only open to the public on a limited basis, so reservations are required for ALL of their programs. Therefore, plan ahead! You'll find it well worth the small extra effort in order to visit. All tours are guided. Offerings include two-hour public tours, field trips, one-hour dolphin encounters with dolphin interaction programs, scenic bayou tours with kayaking, birthday parties, a "Dozing with Dolphins" sleepover, week-long *Ocean Expo Summer Camps*, and *Job Shadowing.* The website www.imms.org is a tool worth studying prior to booking a visit. Well designed and easy to navigate, the website provides helpful descriptions for each of the programs. Prices vary widely for the tours and programs, from under $10 to over $100. All of the programs and tours have limitations on group sizes, and some have age limitations. Save $5 by booking your visit online rather than by phone. An online calendar displays available dates for reservations. Parking is free, and bus parking is available. Summer vacation and holiday dates can fill quickly, so, again, plan ahead.

The Public Tour of the CMER will appeal to visitors of any age. A typical two-hour tour begins in the combination Museum and Gift Shop where you will check in and meet with your friendly guide. After walking next door to a comfortable auditorium, knowledgeable employees, such as Lisa and Skipper, conduct live animal presentations about exotic birds and reptiles. During the *Exotic Bird Presentation*, trained birds are quick to demonstrate their learned behaviors for the audience while the trainer explains about the birds' lives, their training, and the importance of conserving their habitats. The birds' antics frequently have guests laughing. Children respond eagerly to questions from the presenter and guests are given plenty of opportunity to ask questions.

In the *Reptile Program* the audience is drawn into participating as guests are quizzed on their knowledge of marine life, pass around animal specimens in jars, and listen to fascinating stories about sea turtles and other creatures. Near the end of this session, Skipper may bring out an albino snake, named Eve, and invite observers to come pet it.

On to the Discovery Room where no less than a dozen aquariums line the walls displaying sea life from varying types of Gulf Coast environments, including fresh water, brackish water, the Mississippi Sound, and the higher salinity regions of the Gulf. Reptile enclosures in the Discovery Room house marsh turtles, bearded dragons, snakes, and alligators. Large touch pools hold a variety of fascinating sea creatures such as cownose and Atlantic stingrays, bamboo sharks, horseshoe crabs, fish, blue crabs, sea stars and sea urchins. Guests are welcome to reach in and gently touch horseshoe crabs, rays and sharks. CMER employees are on hand to answer questions and oversee the safe handling of the animals. Josh, one such attendant, explained that many of the animals have affectionately been given names by employees. "Phoenix," "Oscar," and "Yoshi" are among the bamboo sharks, while "Emerson" and "Lily" are names given to a couple of rays. The smallest ray is called, very fittingly, "Pancake."

After the Discovery Room, the tour returns to the 2,000 square foot Museum and Gift Shop. Life-sized replicas of sea creatures hang from the ceiling in this room. Detailed displays reveal facts, such as the differences between porpoises and dolphins, and how marine animals are rescued. Amateur archaeologists will love the "Fossil Dig" sand table. Here, guests sift through sand to uncover a shark tooth, fossilized shells, stingray barbs, or possibly a puffer fish mouth plate. Your guide will help you identify your "find" and mount it on a small card for you to take home. Marine-inspired artwork done in various media is also included in both the Museum and the Gift Shop. You can even purchase a small, simple painting done by one of the CMER's resident dolphins!

If the weather permits, a dolphin presentation is included in the tour. Atlantic Bottlenose dolphins, Bo and Buster, are the featured mammals for the presentation as they work with their trainers in their 65,000-gallon tank. These older, gentle dolphins are retired from the U.S. Navy. As the dolphins perform various behaviors for their trainers, who are in the water with them, another CMER employee narrates facts and stories about the animals for the audience. Did you know that dolphins have bellybuttons? The CMER is also home to a couple of younger rescued dolphins, named "Apollo" and "CJ."

There are two specialized dolphin programs for a real "hands-on" experience: the *Dolphin Encounter* and the *Dolphin Interaction*. Each lasts about one hour and begins with a safety briefing, followed by a presentation on the facility and dolphins. During the *Dolphin Encounter* ($50 per person), the guest kneels near the dock edge to meet one of the dolphins face-to-face. The guest will feed and pet one of the Atlantic Bottlenose dolphins. The participant never enters the water for this adventure. During the *Dolphin Interaction* ($95), also known as "Take a Dip with a Dolphin Program," the guest will actually enter the shallow water with the dolphin to feed, touch and request different behaviors from the dolphin. For an additional $15, you can have a photo taken of yourself with the dolphin. These two dolphin programs are seasonal, offered only from May to October, weather permitting. There are minimum age and height requirements detailed online. A paid adult must accompany the youngest ages allowed. Although a bit on the pricey side for some, the chance to touch or interact with these dolphins is an once-in-a-lifetime experience that will be long remembered.

Field trips for school groups are very similar to the Public Tours. In addition to the Discovery Room, museum and animal presentations, the field trip may also include an additional educational activity, such as a "Rescue Relay," where students may simulate a dolphin rescue. Instructors and parents are encouraged to visit the website for free lesson plans and fun activity sheets that will enhance any youngster's visit.

The CMER offers several specialized programs ranging from teaching participants fishing techniques to exploring a bayou by kayak. A minimum of ten participants is required.

For anglers age five and older, the three-hour fishing course ($12 per person) provides a great introduction to the art and science of fishing. Try your hand at basic rod and reel techniques or give throwing a cast net a whirl. Baiting crab traps is yet another way to tempt a catch. Learn about fish anatomy and how to prepare fish fillets. Contact Chris Breazeale at 228-896-9182 ext. 1767 or chris@imms.org.

If "eco-adventures" appeal to you, consider viewing nature up close from the seat of a two-person kayak. Two educator-guides will accompany your group through Bayou Bernard to see various habitats and species of birds and other wildlife as you glide through the water. The three-hour trip ($30 per person) is offered on first and third Saturdays of each month, April through October, weather permitting. Contact Dennis McGrury at 228-896-9182 ext. 1772 or dmcgrury@imms.org.

For those who might prefer relaxing to paddling during their bayou tour, a three-hour "Scenic Bayou Tour" on a twenty-four-passenger pontoon boat is a great alternative. Floating through Biloxi's Back Bay, the Mississippi Sound, or the Tchoutacabouffa River, you'll explore differing habitats, providing opportunities for wonderful nature photos. Reserve a morning, afternoon, or sunset cruise. The cost is $30 for adults and $24 for children ages eight-twelve. The minimum number of fifteen guests is required for the cruise to be scheduled. A 10% discount on tickets is offered for those booking the entire boat. A non-refundable deposit is required. Contact Chris Breazeale at 228-896-9182 ext. 1767 or chris@imms.org.

A birthday party can be extra special by hosting it at the CMER. For $305 and up, depending on the package options you choose, you and up to thirty party guests can enjoy use of a pre-decorated party room with utensils, plates and napkins provided. Activities include a private tour of the museum complete with a "dig," interaction with aquatic life in the touch-pool room, and a dolphin presentation. Your birthday child will receive a "Birthday Shirt." All you need to bring is the cake and ice cream! The ninety-minute parties are scheduled for morning or afternoon. Add-ons can include live bird presentations, rather than the touch-pool, and petting the dolphins versus just viewing them for an additional fee. Call or reserve online; with only three party rooms, the calendar fills quickly!

Looking for an extra exciting event for your youth group or family reunion? How about a sleepover that is interactive, educational and a blast? Originally designed by an Eagle Scout for scouting groups, the "Dozing with Dolphins" program can be easily adjusted for the requirements of many types of groups. During your overnight stay, you'll watch a movie on the big screen, feed live animals, enjoy a behind-the-scenes tour, observe animal training presentations and more. Guests will receive a participation patch as a memento. Breakfast is provided in the morning. The "Dozing with Dolphins" program is available the second and fourth Fridays of the month, except during November and December, when only second Fridays are scheduled. The cost is $18 for adults and $25 for children.

Okay, not many kids would get excited if you told them that their summer vacation might be spent attending "educational" camps. However, the Institute for Marine Mammal Studies has managed to take all the pain out of learning and inject it with a good dose of plain, old fun. Youngsters age 5-14 flock to the week-long tuition-based Ocean Expo Summer Camps that operate Monday through Friday, from 8:30am-3:30pm, beginning each June. There's not much time spent sitting around in classrooms as the campers learn about various aquatic habitats and the creatures that live in them. Whether aboard the IMMS' *Curlew* or on the beach, plenty of focused activity and hands-on participation keep the kids tuned in as they explore nature. Seining, sieving, beach combing, fishing, crabbing, dissecting, and performing water quality tests are among the planned adventures. Older campers may visit Ship Island or go kayaking. After attending a couple of the Ocean Expo Summer Camps, one thirteen-year-old young lady named Kaya was asked to describe the experience. With an obvious glow of fondness, she responded simply, "Awesome!" Camp tuition varies by age from $170-$230 per week. A limited number of scholarships are available. Registration forms and a five-page *Parent Handbook* can be obtained through links on the website "Summer Camp" page.

Students considering a future as a marine biologist, an animal trainer, a veterinarian, or any similar career at a marine education and research facility should be aware that the IMMS offers a *Job Shadow* program for $75. Learn what a typical work day might be like in this field as you "shadow" a staff member for an afternoon. Ask questions about how to best prepare for the job or, perhaps, the best and worst aspects of the career that you are considering. Discover early whether a career in this field might be for you! Individuals must be twelve years or older for this program. Reservations can be booked for Tuesday-Friday from 12:30pm-3:30pm. Make your reservations today by calling 228-896-9182.

If you are over eighteen, you can volunteer or apply for an internship. This is a terrific idea for both those volunteers who simply love nature and are able to give of their time to help promote the IMMS mission, or for those students who want a bit of early experience in this career field. Melissa, a soft-spoken young woman with a beautiful smile, grew up with a love for working with animals. As a youngster, she spent many of her after-school hours working with horses at nearby stables, and her summers attending classes at Sea World. When she reached college age, she chose to volunteer at the CMER as she fulfilled requirements for her psychology degree. Now, as a full-time IMMS employee, Melissa leads tour groups through the facility. Her passion for what she does is apparent when she speaks about the animals. When asked what her favorite part of her job might be, she replied, "Being able to help educate people and knowing that I've made a difference."

Should you be planning an event, whether for your organization, business or family, consider renting space at the CMER. It is conveniently located within an hour of New Orleans and Mobile, and close to both the interstate and the Gulfport International Airport. The brand new facility has a 180-seat auditorium for meetings or presentations. Both high-speed Internet and A/V equipment are available. The museum, with its fascinating exhibits and art-covered walls, provides a unique place to gather. Call for pricing and reservations.

The Gulf Coast is blessed with this incredible scientific, educational, and recreational facility. With all the opportunities it offers for visitors and residents of all ages, it's a jewel not to be missed!

With great appreciation to Melissa, Martha, and Kaya Welsh, Skipper Talley, and Mike Mashburn for their generous help and boundless patience as they answered so many questions by phone, email, and in interviews.

Institute for Marine Mammal Studies
Website: http://www.imms.org
10801 Dolphin Lane, Gulfport, MS 39503
Phone: 228-896-9182
Fax: 228-896-9183
Email: contactus@imms.org
Field Trip: mmashburn@imms.org

Beauvoir

Anne McKee – Meridian, MS

The ghosts of the giant oak trees that grace the Beauvoir property seem to whisper in stilted and breathless words, "She is a survivor."

Indeed, she is.

The graceful mansion sits face-to-face with the Gulf of Mexico, finding the breezes off the Gulf not a threat, but welcomed as renewals of life. Beauvoir has seen war and defeat, loss and love, heartbreaks and triumphs, and she continues to boldly take her place in history – a place designated for survivors. The survival of Beauvoir, itself, has been a story of destiny.

James Brown first purchased the property for $900 in cash, plus a note for $1,100 paid upon receipt of the clear title. He planned a place of beauty and rest for his family. Originally intended as the summer home of the James Brown Family, construction on the main building began in 1848, with completion in 1852. The charming house was constructed with cypress lumber from the nearby Back Bay swamps and the slate for the roof imported from England, creating a sanctuary of peace and harmony. When Mrs. Dorsey purchased the property in 1873 she named the lovely mansion Beauvoir, which means "beautiful to view" in French. She, too, planned a retreat to provide a peaceful atmosphere.

It was in 1876 when Beauvoir's destiny became apparent. At that time Sarah Dorsey gained information that the former president of the Confederacy, Jefferson Davis and family, actively sought a place of quiet and rest, where he could pen his memoirs. She invited him to visit Beauvoir and he arrived in December. The beauty of the live oaks, magnolias, and cedars captivated the war-torn former president of the Confederacy.

Mrs. Dorsey helped Davis to write his manuscript that eventually became *The Rise and Fall of the Confederate Government.* Mrs. Dorsey was very accomplished in her own right. Her written work was serialized in 1863 in the *Southern Literary Messenger* and published in book form in 1869, with additional works published between 1863 and 1879.

During the writing of the book, many former Confederate leaders came to Beauvoir to be interviewed by Jefferson Davis. In one of these interviews with General Jubal A. Early, Mrs. Dorsey learned Davis was almost destitute. Mrs. Dorsey informed Early that she was very ill and planned to leave her entire estate to Davis, but he was not to know or he would not permit her plans.

Mrs. Davis arrived to Beauvoir from Europe in October 1877 and soon became enthralled with the book project. She commented in a letter about Mrs. Dorsey a few weeks after her arrival, "She makes us very comfortable … I am very fond of her."

Mrs. Dorsey offered to sell Beauvoir to Jefferson Davis in February of 1879. A deal was struck for the amount of $5,500 to be paid in three installments, after which Mrs. Dorsey moved to New Orleans. She died of cancer in the early morning of July 4, 1879.

In her will, she stated:

I owe no obligation of any sort whatsoever to any relative of my own. I have done all I could for them … I, therefore, give and bequeath all of my property, real, personal, and mixed, wherever located and situated, wholly and entirely, without hindrance or qualifications, to my most honored and esteemed friend, Jefferson Davis, ex-president of the Confederate States, for his sole use and, in fee simple forever, and I hereby constitute him my sole heir, executive and administrator. If Jefferson Davis should not survive me, I give all that I have bequeathed to him to his youngest daughter, Varina. I do not intend to share in the ingratitude of my country towards the man, who is in my eyes, the highest and noblest in existence.

Eventually Jefferson Davis completed the two-volume book set, in which he, Mrs. Dorsey, and Mrs. Davis each had contributed to the research and writing, during the time they lived in Biloxi.

Davis died in 1889, and Beauvoir was passed to daughter, Winnie, who was a writer as well and became known as "The Daughter of the Confederacy." When she died in 1898, the home was left to Mrs. Davis, who moved two years later to New York. In 1903, Beauvoir was sold to the Mississippi Division, Sons of Confederate Veterans, for the sum of $10,000, much less than Mrs. Davis had been offered previously by a hotel corporation, who had offered $90,000. Mrs. Davis sold the property for the lesser amount, with the stipulation that it would be operated as a Confederate soldier's home, and the house dedicated to the memory of her husband.

From 1903 to 1957 approximately 2,500 veterans and families

lived on the Beauvoir property sustained by a dozen barrack buildings, a hospital, and a chapel behind the main house. When they died, these veterans were buried on the property in a Confederate Veterans Cemetery, whose markers still today create an endearing monument to their efforts. Today only the walls of Beauvoir can tell the tales of the war stories as told by the veterans. Those stories were relived as a time in American history that were too bloody and graphic for the general public to understand, but because their leader and family had once walked the grounds of the gentle house that sat among the great oak trees, perhaps the veterans' sorrowful memories were eased by the comfort of that knowledge.

The destiny of Beauvoir continued. The mansion that was "beautiful to view" offered a balm of healing to those war heroes, when they had nothing else. By the efforts of Mrs. Jefferson Davis and her daughter, Winnie, their husband and father was remembered in a way so needed by the survivors of the "cruel, cruel war." The mother and daughter had the great hope that Ex-President Davis would be honored and memorialized as a man who bravely performed his duty during desperate times, when called upon by his Southern neighbors and constituents.

It was with a heavy heart for his surviving family, and those dedicated veterans who remained, to know that when he died in 1889, the Ex-President died without a country. After the Great American Civil War ended in 1865, Davis was taken prisoner and released after two years, but never regained his United States citizenship. It wasn't until 1978, that then President Jimmy Carter signed into law a resolution of Congress restoring to citizenship the last Confederate.

The mansion's destiny continued to offer a home for the homeless, to comfort the heartbroken, to supply a place for weary heads to rest, and to smile upon those who thought their broken lives were over. The giant oaks, the Gulf's breeze, and the reassuring presence of those who had come before – all were part of that destiny.

The year 1941 marked the opening of the main house for public tours, and, as well, eventually a Confederate Museum, Jefferson Davis Gallery, gift shop, the Tomb of the Unknown Confederate Soldier, and the Jefferson Davis Presidential Library and Museum. Although the mansion was no longer a home for the Confederate soldiers, Beauvoir had continued its destiny as a survivor.

The fateful year of 2005 brought a disaster to the Mississippi Gulf Coast by the hurricane known as Katrina. Thousands of homes and businesses were destroyed or horrifically damaged. Unbelievably, the main house was not totally destroyed, although all of the outbuildings were demolished. Some thought it was gone forever, but that's not Beauvoir's style.

The main body of the home survived primarily due to the substance of the three-inch solid cedar floors. Amazingly many pieces of the furnishings survived, including some furniture, drapes, paintings, lamps, and china. Even after a foot of water, the grandfather clock, used by Davis, only needed a good cleaning and adjustment to retain the chiming of accurate time. Also, the beautiful dining room furniture sits ready for the next meal to be served, just as it did in 1879.

You will notice that in the corner of each room an area is purposely left unfinished in order to gleam a glance of the original color and design. During the post-Katrina restoration process, a leading historical-color analyst determined the original color, which was found under seven layers of paint. Today we are fortunate to see and enjoy the same colors as were seen by the Brown, Dorsey, and Davis families.

Today as the mansion has been completely restored, hope thrives once again. The stunning views of the Gulf are still there. There are gardens, walking paths, memorials and the Confederate Veterans

Cemetery. It is interesting to know on June 3, 2008, Jefferson Davis' 200th Birthday, Beauvoir was fully restored and reopened for public tours. The mansion may be seen today in the original condition at the time of President and Varina Davis.

By the winter of 2009, President Davis's personal library was rebuilt and opened for tours. Later that year work began on the Jefferson Davis Presidential Library. Additional planned renovations include the historic kitchen, veterans' barracks, as well as replicas and additional outbuildings are to be built.

It is estimated about sixty percent of the original papers stored in the house pertaining to American Civil War history and the United Confederate Veterans and the Sons of Confederate Veterans organizations are salvageable. These include photographs, personal letters, manuscripts, envelopes, postcards, newspaper clippings and various records of that era. The reconstruction of the mansion, outbuildings, and grounds continue through the efforts of many civilian volunteers, the Mississippi Army National Guard, and additional lovers of history who have ardently brought the mansion back to life.

The work will continue because the destiny is still there. What will the next one hundred years bring to Beauvoir? The first hundred and eighty years have had stories of a sense of place that will not die. There are stories from the whispering giant oaks; stories from the sometimes destructive, sometimes comforting ocean breezes;

the moans of battle-worn warriors; the accounts of courage and inspiration to tell and record for all of those who will come later, year-after-year, decade-after-decade. Yes, the Beauvoir destiny continues.

Come and be a part of the continuing story of Beauvoir. Listen to the echoes of bygone voices. Walk the pathways of the brave-hearted-survivors. Breathe the salty air and enjoy the splash of the ocean waves – all healing and encouraging. Life goes on … Beauvoir lives.

Beauvoir is owned and operated by the Mississippi Division of Sons of Confederate Veterans.

Timeline:

1848 – 1873 James Brown Years

1873 – 1879 Sarah Dorsey Years

1877 – 1989 Davis Family Years

1889 – 1903 Mrs. Davis & Winnie's ownership

1903 – 1957 Confederate Veterans Home

1941 – Present Beauvoir open for tours

Beauvoir location: 2244 Beach Blvd., Biloxi, MS
Open for tours Monday through Sunday, 9:00 am to 5:00 pm
Website: http://www.beauvoir.org
Phone: 228-338-4400

Dancing with the Trees: The Ohr-O'Keefe Museum of Art

Patti Carr Black and Denny Mecham

Ten years in the making, the Ohr-O'Keefe Museum of Art celebrates the innovative, independent, and creative spirit of namesake Mississippi master potter George Ohr. In a fitting tribute to Ohr, architect Frank Gehry designed an award winning campus of five bold, self-sufficient structures which offer separate but not isolated experiences - together creating a single unified vision connected by an expansive brick plaza and majestic live oaks. Each of the buildings, individually and collectively, serves aspects of the Museum's mission and programming: the Mississippi Sound Welcome Center, the IP Casino Resort Spa Exhibitions Gallery, the Gallery of African American Art, the City of Biloxi Center for Ceramics, and the John S. and James L. Knight Gallery, home of the permanent exhibition on the work and life of George Edgar Ohr.

The Ohr-O'Keefe Museum of Art honors the lives of three disparate men who made unique contributions to Biloxi: George Ohr, potter; Frank Gehry, contemporary architect; and Pleasant Reed, freedman carpenter.

George Ohr (1857-1918) was born in Biloxi soon after his parents arrived as emigrants from Germany and Alsace (France), through the port of New Orleans. His father established the first blacksmith shop in Biloxi, and later, the first grocery store. Ohr tried out a number of trades before a friend introduced him to pottery-making in 1879. It changed his life. For two years he traveled the United

States visiting potteries and museums to learn all he could about art pottery.

In 1883, the self-proclaimed "Mad Potter of Biloxi" came home to build his own pottery shop. With his blacksmithing skills, he fabricated all of the ironwork, made the potter's wheel, built the kiln, rafted lumber down river, sawed it into boards, and built his shop. Ready to begin making his wares, he rowed his skiff up the Tchoutacabouffa River, dug and loaded the clay, and brought it back to his shop. At first he had to concentrate on making a living with items such as coffee mugs, puzzles, flowerpots, pitchers, and flue pipes for fireplaces. His intention, however, was to create art pottery and exhibit his work as widely as possible. He soon began producing unusual shapes that he glazed with experimental combinations.

He exhibited over 600 pots at the 1885 fair in New Orleans. For a few years he divided his time working at the New Orleans Art Pottery and at his own shop in Biloxi. In a short time his Biloxi Art and Novelty Pottery had become a tourist attraction, crammed with vessels of all shapes, sizes, and decorations. As he created his pots, he created himself into a wildly eccentric persona, imbuing his business with show-biz hype. Fascinated visitors would watch him in a virtuoso performance at the potter's wheel and buy a memento of their trip. In 1894 his shop was destroyed by fire. Within months Ohr had rebuilt his pottery with a five-story tower shaped like a pagoda painted bright pink. He called it Biloxi Art Pottery Unlimited, and there he stepped up his experimentation in throwing extremely thin-walled, delicate pots that he manipulated into exotic forms by twisting, denting, ruffling, and folding the clay. His pottery was exhibited at the American World's Fair of 1893, 1895, 1901, 1904 and 1905. His peers were aware of his talents, but the public was not attracted to his pieces. He gave up his profession in 1909, disappointed that he was not recognized as the genius he knew himself to be. He refused to sell individual pieces of his art pottery. He packed up over 7,000 items in 1910. Ohr died in 1918.

Ohr's work was discovered by the art world a half-century after his death. An antiques dealer from New Jersey bought the cache of pots and when they began circulating among art pottery collectors, a new star was born. Ohr has been called the first American artist to produce abstract art. He pushed form beyond the functional to the sculptural and presaged the sensibility of color and form that became abstract expressionism in the 1950s.

Frank Gehry is an internationally acclaimed architect, winner of major awards in his field for his wildly creative and thoughtful architecture. Born in Canada in 1929, he moved with his family to California and earned his architectural degree from the University of Southern California. Among his important buildings across the globe are museums in Spain, Germany, France, the Czech Republic, Canada, and the United States.

To understand Gehry's work is to understand his interest in coming to Biloxi to create a museum for George Ohr's pottery. At first sight the works of both men seem like playful geometrics, free imaginations at work pursuing ideas beyond traditional technical constraints, and daring beyond aesthetic norms. Yet the works of both men show total control and assurance. They shared an interest in testing the traditional conceptions of form and perceived the possibilities inherent in the use of conventional materials. Both experimented with new orders: Gehry introducing radical architectural elements; Ohr soaring beyond the forms of the art pottery of his day.

Gehry's most recent building, his first skyscraper in New York, was unveiled in 2011. Called "New York by Gehry," at 8 Spruce Street in Manhattan, it is the largest apartment building in the Western hemisphere. Here again we can see in Gehry's work impulses similar to those of Ohr. On the exterior of this building Gehry used twisted steel to resemble soft, crumpled fabric. In the inverse, more than a century earlier, Ohr created soft folded vessel forms and glazed them to resemble metal. In both processes the artists made their basic materials sensuous, alive with energy and movement. Their unexpected shapes and surfaces produced sculptural forms never before seen in architecture or pottery. The lives of both men are paeans to individuality and creative imagination. Both men shattered traditions in their medium.

The Museum was first located in the George E. Ohr Cultural Center with the public library, adjacent to Biloxi's City Hall. By 1998, a capital campaign to construct a new museum on Beach Blvd had begun. Frank O. Gehry and Gehry Partners LLP began the architectural design process in 1998, completing it in 2003.

Construction began at the present site in 2004. In five short years, the organization grew from a small community operation with a narrow frame of reference to plans for a stunning $35 million dollar 21st century museum with a much larger regional, national, and international audience. With the intriguing combination personalities of aesthetic iconoclasts George Ohr and Frank Gehry, the national media followed the progress of the project with articles in *Smithsonian Magazine*, *Architectural Digest*, *The New York Times,* and *Los Angeles Times* as well as regional coverage.

One of the buildings on the Ohr Museum campus is the Pleasant Reed Home. Pleasant Reed (1854-1936) was born enslaved on John B. Reed's plantation near Hattiesburg. He was still a child when the Emancipation Proclamation was signed in 1863. Soon after the Civil War ended, his family moved to the Coast to start a new life. Reed was fourteen when he arrived in Biloxi and began work in the building trades, becoming a successful and skillful carpenter. Reed labored under the restrictions placed on African-Americans by the Jim Crow laws that came into effect around 1880. It took him over two decades to build his own house because he could not borrow money to complete it all at one time. His wife worked as a domestic in the community, and Reed learned to make fishing nets as a second trade to support their six children. Their family became respected citizens in the City of Biloxi.

Reed's carpentry was utilitarian by necessity, but it reflects the talent, energy, and efficacy of his efforts. His 1400 square foot home was moved to the Ohr-O'Keefe campus in 2002 to assure its preservation. Destroyed by Hurricane Katrina three years later, the present reconstruction of the original house was completed in 2010. The Pleasant Reed Interpretive Center provides an educational experience in African-American history and, through Reed's careful work in the traditional, local style, a look at urban architecture of nineteenth century Biloxi.

On August 29, 2005, Hurricane Katrina severely damaged both the new construction as well as the George E. Ohr Cultural Center that housed the Museum at that time. Fortunately, the Museum's art and artifacts were stored prior to the storm and survived without damage. With normalcy on the Gulf Coast at a halt for an unknown period, the collection was then relegated to more permanent storage while the Board of Trustees evaluated the situation. In 2006, the Board committed to re-building. Construction began anew in 2008 at the beachfront site and by 2014 the campus was completed. Just as Ohr (1857-1918) rose from devastating personal and professional loss to create an extraordinary body of work, so too the Ohr-O'Keefe has risen from Katrina's destruction, a homage to the enduring human spirit.

The Ohr-O'Keefe Museum:
386 Beach Blvd., Biloxi, MS
Phone: 228-374-5547
Website: http://www.georgeohr.org

The Friendship Oak at The University of Southern Mississippi Gulf Park Campus

Jamie O'Quinn – Hattiesburg, MS

The rise and fall of the Friendship Oak's sturdy limbs mirror the movement of the Gulf of Mexico, its nautical counterpart a few hundred feet away. Just like the tide, the roots of this famous live oak sometimes ride high, often dip low, and mostly have remained deep and hidden over the course of time. Its lower branches have never been trimmed, for this ancient tree grew in its natural state with twisting tentacle looking limbs before the first powerful saw ever came to this continent. Such began the ebb and flow history of the Friendship Oak, a Mississippi Gulf Coast icon whose birth has been estimated at 1487, five years before Columbus discovered the New World.

Under the shady canvas of this sprawling fifty-nine feet tall conifer with its 155 feet crown spread, Dr. James Pat Smith, Professor of History at The University of Southern Mississippi Gulf Coast, shared some of the history of the tree, the area, and the school.

Nicholas Ladner, a descendant of a French salt prisoner, and his wife, Mary Ann, obtained a Spanish land grant for this area after their home and cattle were wiped off Cat Island by a hurricane in the 1790s. The Ladners reestablished themselves near the Friendship Oak where they built an old-fashioned country cabin with chimneys on both ends that looked over the water around where St. Thomas

Church now stands. The two tall chimneys on their home soon became a navigational halfway marker for steamboats and other nautical traffic going up and down the coast between Mobile and New Orleans. The spot carried the name "The Chimneys" well into the 1900s.

John McCaughan eventually purchased the property and built Rosalie mansion, thus giving the name Rosalie to the first official town, later renamed Long Beach. Loving this place, McCaughan is said to have buried the heads of sharks and other fish he didn't want to eat around the oak trees to help them prosper. Eventually becoming a state senator and the first postmaster of Biloxi, John and his father-in-law bought up land back on the east end of the coast and incorporated a town they called Mississippi City, now part of Gulfport. McCaughan went to the legislature and had Harrison County carved out of Hancock and Jackson Counties and put the courthouse on his property on Courthouse Road. McCaughan and his father-in-law would sit on the property near the Friendship Oak and dream about what has now become the three legs of the Mississippi Gulf Coast economy: tourism, the railroads and port, and higher education.

While in the senate, McCaughan fought to have Mississippi's first state public university established, and once the idea was accepted, he was on the committee to decide where to build it. Assured that enough votes were in place for Mississippi City to be chosen as the university's site, the decision to locate it there was lost by one vote and it went to Oxford instead. "There in the legislature, when McCaughan realized he had been double crossed on the vote, he beat the double crossing legislator with his cane," Smith said. "Upon returning home, he started organizing a drive for the bottom three counties to secede from Mississippi and affix themselves to Louisiana. That drive was short lived. Eventually he was appointed to the Board of Trustees at the University of Mississippi. After McCaughan's death, the community, which is today called Long Beach, continued to grow and began to be known as a truck and farming area and self-acclaimed Radish Capital of the World.

"Before the World War I era, some of the more prominent and wealthy people in the community became concerned about the lack of higher education for their children, so they brought in Colonel

Hardy, who had created boys' schools all across the country," per Dr. Smith. Hardy helped establish the Gulf Coast Military Academy, an all-boys school, at Mississippi City further down the coast, which included high school through junior college curriculum. The Academy stayed in existence until the devastation of Hurricane Camille in 1969, and after it closed the site was used by William Carey College until Hurricane Katrina ravished the community. "As the Gulf Coast Military Academy got off the ground, people started asking Hardy about starting a girls' school for their daughters. Hardy was not interested, stating he knew nothing about the education of women, for at that time there was still a rigid notion that males and females should be educated in different ways." Indeed women were seen as too anxious to withstand the more stressful, harder part of curriculum as compared to their male counterparts. With a bit more encouragement, however, Hardy finally agreed to take on establishing a girls' school and, doing what he knew best, he used the same curriculum for the girls as he had for the boys.

Though it came well after his death, McCaughan's dream of having a university in his community came to fruition as the Gulf Park College for Women was established and the greatest of his beloved oak trees, today known as the Friendship Oak, became a centerpiece for the campus. "The term Friendship Oak originates back to the 1920s when this campus began as the Gulf Park College for Women. It was a four-year women's school, teaching eleventh and twelfth grades and the first two years of college. The students designated the space under this tree as a private spot to meet, an area from which administration and faculty were banned," Smith explained. "It was during these freer discussions that strong bonds were forged and gave birth to the tree's name and legend which states, 'I am called the Friendship Oak. Those who enter my shadow will remain friends through all their lifetime.'"

One of the favorite spots of the tree for students, faculty, and visitors to enjoy was the Treehouse, which was wiped away during the devastation of Hurricane Katrina in 2005. A great place for socializing and even having classes, the Treehouse was a large platform with steps and banister built among the Friendship Oak's branches during the time of the College for Women. "In the 1920s, noted Poet Vachel Lindsay came from New York to teach poetry. He was the first to hold classes in the Treehouse," Smith states.

Alumni of the school possess fond memories of other special occasions under the Friendship Oak, such as gathering of the seniors to pass on their artifacts and sailor hats down to underclass women. After the College for Women closed in 1971, The University of Southern Mississippi took over the campus and continued using the Treehouse. Smith stated that when he came on full time in 1991 there were only a few professors in Arts & Letters. "Whenever someone would get an article published, we would go up to the Treehouse and smoke a cigar," he reported. He credits one of his colleagues with providing a particularly distasteful cigar for personally breaking him of that habit.

As unusual as passing of a sailor hat to an underclasswoman during the pre-World War II era might sound, it actually made great sense, for this college for women was not ordinary, but rather quite radical for the time. Smith said, "They took literature, Latin, math, and participated in non-traditional physical activities including learning to sail, riding horses, and learning to canoe. Their activities were very rigorous."

During the 1930s learning to fly was added to their list. A local Mississippi Gulf Coast African-American war hero airman, named John C. Robinson, would fly back home to Gulfport periodically and help raise money for his church, St. Paul African Methodist Episcopal Church in Gulfport. Among the people who flew with him at the old Gulfport field was Dr. Cox, President at Gulf Park College for Women. "Cox was so taken with the flight that he decided that flying would be an interesting optional activity for the girls. He wanted his students to learn about the technology of the future and arranged for those who were interested to take lessons with a local flight instructor at Gulfport field."

Due to the damage of Hurricane Camille in 1969, Gulf Park College for Women closed its doors. The University of Southern Mississippi Gulf Park took over the campus and still thrives today. Though the Treehouse no longer exists, the shade of the Friendship Oak continues to be a favorite gathering place for socializing, studying, and special events for students, faculty, alumni and the community. According to Professor Smith, "Just this past Saturday, we had a couple get married here under the tree and use the canvas for their wedding location. Tour buses continue to make this a regular stop as well." With a trunk diameter of 6 feet 2.75 inches and trunk circumference of 19 feet 9.5 inches, there is still plenty of room to rest in the shadow of the Friendship Oak. This majestic Gulf Coast icon awaits to welcome yet another friend to join the legend that many have treasured for a lifetime.

University of Southern Mississippi Gulf Park Campus
730 East Beach Blvd., Long Beach, MS 39560
Phone: 228-865-4500

Infinity Space Center

Ellis Anderson – Bay St. Louis, MS

Quick. Name four scientific centers that have been key in America's space program. There's Cape Canaveral in Florida, and Johnson Space Center in Houston. And, oh yes, the US Space & Rocket Center in Huntsville, Alabama. But number four? Time's up! The buzzer goes off and the answer appears: *Hancock County, Mississippi.*

Wait. *Mississippi?*

Few people realize the Stennis Space Center (SSC) - one of the largest scientific centers in the world - calls the Gulf Coast of Mississippi home. Now, the new INFINITY Science Center gives the public an introduction to some of the exciting work taking place at SSC. Located just outside the gates of the restricted access space center, INFINITY sits near the Louisiana / Mississippi border. The striking glass building rises up from the forest alongside Mississippi's I-10 looking as if it belongs to the future. And it does, because while INFINITY acts as a window onto Stennis, its main mission is one of inspiration.

Both inside and out at the science center, budding scientists and engineers are able to explore the galaxies of space, the bottoms of the ocean, and the mysterious beauty of the Gulf Coast wetlands. The entire educational center is designed to launch future generations of scientists, engineers, and mathematicians.

And launch them it has. INFINITY first opened its doors in the spring of 2012, and the 10,000 square foot $10 million dollar facility welcomed over 65,000 visitors the first year of operation. But it's obvious that children aren't the only ones to catch "space fever" at INFINITY – the science center fires up imaginations of every age.

The fun starts even before entering the space-age building. The sweeping entrance plaza features a towering eagle sculpture created from an ancient oak tree and steel recycled from a Space Shuttle engine. Dotting the plaza are buoys, riverine craft, and rocket engines, like the F-1 rocket engine that powered Apollo flights to the moon, one of the biggest engines built in human history.

Once inside the door, visitors are greeted by a video of astronaut Fred Haise. Haise is now retired and serves as vice-chairman of the INFINITY board, but in 1970 the Biloxi native was one of three astronauts aboard the Apollo 13 expedition. Their mission was to explore the surface of the moon. Equipment failure turned the spacecraft into a "lifeboat." For three days, a breathless world watched news reports of the astronauts' struggle to survive. The crew remained undaunted and, against great odds, piloted the ship safely back to earth. In 1995 the account of that drama was detailed in the box-office hit movie "Apollo 13."

Haise has spent over a decade helping establish the science center. He believes that INFINITY can help revolutionize science education and inspire future explorers to pursue careers in science, technology, engineering, and math.

The first exhibit visitors see inside INFINITY, *Great Nations Dare to Explore,* is an immersive, hands-on experience offering "time-travel" with history's great explorers. Visitors even get a sneak peek at what colonies might some day look like on the moon and Mars.

Moving on into the immersive theater, *Science on a Sphere*, uses a state-of-the-art computer with four projectors to show revolving, animated views of Earth's atmosphere, geography, and weather patterns. The Sphere also takes visitors millions of miles to the seething surface of the Sun and to the mysterious red planet Mars.

Just outside the theater awe-inspiring rocket models (one over thirty feet tall) rise toward the vaulted ceiling, while an exciting

Hurricane Simulator will raise hair – literally – with winds up to seventy-eight miles per hour. Visitors can reach the Space Gallery upstairs by the sweeping staircase or the space-age glass elevator that looks like a rocket. If you're in the company of children, expect to take the elevator ride at least a few times during your visit, even though the stairs are close at hand.

In the *Space Gallery* upstairs, exhibits show how space travel has evolved over the past fifty years. One star feature is a full-sized module of the International Space Station. A video features former astronaut Scott Altman in a tour of the space station, explaining the everyday life of astronauts who currently live and work nearly 250 miles above the Earth.

Back downstairs in the *Earth Gallery*, visitors can experience space travel in the Omega Flight Simulator ($5 tickets are discounted for groups of twenty or more). The high-tech thrill ride uses the same technology used to train professional pilots, with an HD big-screen experience.

In the coming years look for even more exciting exhibits. The center's long-range expansion plans were fast-tracked when Mississippi's governor, Phil Bryant, announced that another $10 million from the BP Deepwater Horizon Oil Spill Early Restoration Fund Agreement will be used to build new indoor/outdoor exhibits and interpretive centers at INFINITY and the surrounding area. Future exhibits include a series of high-tech interactive labs in the center's *Earth Gallery*, where kids and adults can learn about the value of the Gulf Coast ecosystem, as well as topics like ocean exploration, global observation, and remote sensing.

INFINITY will provide both researchers and the public the opportunity to monitor a $50 million "Living Shoreline" project in Hancock County (also funded by an Early Restoration Project). The six-mile living shoreline will consist of a natural and artificial breakwater material to stabilize highly eroded areas and provide habitat for shrimp, oysters, and fish.

While the *Living Shoreline* will create both fishing and shrimping opportunities, its main job is to help build and restore crucial marsh areas of the shoreline. The data gathered and monitored at INFINITY will create more understanding about the importance of the Gulf Coast ecosystem and foster appreciation of natural resources.

Also on the horizon are a series of defined "missions," where both children and adults will be able to learn about the history and ecology of the area. Outside the building, a nature trail is being developed that will lead visitors through the sensitive wetlands areas adjacent to science center.

Bicyclists, hikers, and birders will someday enjoy an enhanced connectivity between INFINITY and Hancock County's beachfront, only ten miles away. Although the Waveland beaches were impacted by the 2010 oil spill, the area is now gaining prominence as a national birding destination. Interpretive learning centers along the trail will link the two destinations.

A free guided bus tour of Stennis Space Center is included in the admission to INFINITY, giving visitors a fascinating behind-the-scenes look at the nation's largest rocket engine testing facility. Testing engines may not seem that glamorous, but it's absolutely essential to the space program. Long before any launch countdown could begin, the enormous engines that have propelled humans and payloads into space over the past fifty years had to be tested repeatedly during development. With nearly 14,000 acres in the complex, and an additional 125,000-acre buffer zone, Stennis has held the keys to outer space. During the race to space in the 60's, a favorite quip was, "If you want to go to the moon, you have to get there through Mississippi."

Over the decades high-tech corporations and other branches of government, besides NASA, have flocked to Stennis Space Center. Today SSC is one of the most unique scientific "cities" in the world.

Over 5,000 people work at the facility, with jobs ranging from rocket science, to ocean mapping, to meteorology.

Back at INFINITY after the tour, visitors will be able to stock up at the science center's gift shop, which carries everything from NASA logo apparel to space toys and games – including real astronaut ice cream treats. If all the exploration has worked up appetites, the restaurant at INFINITY offers dining that's both casual and delicious, in a unique atmosphere that's "out of this world." Both INFINITY's café and gift shop are open without admission to locals and to thousands of travelers who stop at the adjacent I-10 Mississippi Welcome Center each month.

Throughout the year INFINITY offers special programs, such as a space camp for kids in the summer, opportunities to meet working astronauts and scientists, and fun experiment programs that offer hands-on learning experiences. For parents looking for an unforgettable adventure to mark a child's birthday, INFINITY hosts parties for children. The 30,000-square-foot facility can be reserved for special events of all types and features a separate conference area for corporate meetings.

As one of only ten NASA Visitor Centers nationally, INFINITY is included in the "Passport to Space," a free program in which members receive discounts and perks at other space centers across the country. See more details and complete information on INFINITY at www.visitinfinity.com.

Infinity Science Center
Location: South of I-10, Exit 2, just East of the Louisiana/Mississippi Border
Open: Monday - Saturday from 10 am to 4 pm
$10: Adults (Age 18-54) $8: Senior (55+), Military $6: Children (4-17), Ages 3 and under FREE. Group rates available.
Website: http://www.visitinfinity.com

These Properties are NOT Condemned

Historic Revitalization Keeps The Arts Alive on the Coast

Kara Martinez Bachman – Mandeville, LA

Mississippi has a strong interest in telling its stories through restored architectural gems. While it may at times be affordable to build a new modern structure from scratch, it is often the crumbling walls, high ceilings and meaningful history of older buildings that impart the romance that arts and entertainment projects require. Old structures, whether they were originally theaters such as the Saenger in Biloxi, homes such as in Bay St. Louis, or the Ocean Spring High School, have been restored across Mississippi to serve as temples to the arts. They are relics from times when our culture emphasized handcrafted structures meant to last. Many of these buildings, whether accurately restored or retrofitted for modern use, reflect the creative souls of the towns in which they were built.

Everyone was surprised by the turnout on the day the movie stars returned to Bay St. Louis. The historic building on Blaize Avenue in downtown was packed to its rafters with people eager to catch a glimpse of celebrity. It was hot inside, where the floorboards creaked and every spare inch was filled with audience; outside, the overflow covered the walkways. The audience was there to celebrate two things: the grand opening of the new location of the Bay St. Louis Little Theater, and the return to the bay of two actors who had made a mark on both the entertainment industry, as well as on this artsy beachside town. This day, and every day since, has illustrated the important role that historic architectural revitalization plays in the cultural life of towns and cities across the coast.

On that day in October 2011, Academy Award nominated actress Mary Badham sat on the newly renovated theater stage with actor John Provost, and both recounted their days of shooting the 1966 film *This Property is Condemned*, which was based on the one-act play of native Mississippian Tennessee Williams. Starring Natalie Wood and Robert Redford, this drama was partially filmed on-site in and around the neighborhood of the three-story building on Blaize Avenue, not far from the historic Bay St. Louis L&N Train Depot.

Badham, who was given a Best Supporting Actress nomination for her role as Scout in the classic film *To Kill a Mockingbird*, graciously recounted memories of her opening scene, which was shot across the street from the theater, alongside the CSX railroad tracks of old town Bay St. Louis. John Provost, who had also starred as the beloved character "Timmy" in the *Lassie* television series, sat alongside her and waxed nostalgic about times spent filming on the tracks in the stifling heat of South Mississippi. The audience ate it up; some present remembered those days of decades ago when Hollywood came to town and The Bay was turned upside down.

But this is not a story about Hollywood; this is a story about historic revitalization. The building in question is the one that so enamored location scouts that they chose its exterior to represent the Starr Boarding House of this film, which boasted a screenplay written by Francis Ford Coppola. The story of this property, and its subsequent renovation post-Katrina, points to the importance that the revitalization of historic architecture can play in the local culture of a place.

The three-story building was believed to have been erected sometime between 1916 and 1929 (sources disagree on the exact year). Details provided by the Bay St. Louis Little Theater (BSLLT), Hancock County Historical Society, and other sources paint a partial picture of the origins of the building. The cinder-block style bricks used in the building's construction were hand-shaped by Bay St. Louis merchant and original owner of the home, Andreas Scafidi. The historical record shows that the first floor was used as some type of general store, and the upper floors were used to house Scafidi's family during earlier days in The Bay. Over the years, the building was used as everything from a home to a bottling location for Dr. Nut, an amaretto-flavored soft drink headquartered in New Orleans.

The building now housing the BSLLT was originally similar to the Starr Boarding House of the film; in later years it fell into neglect and disrepair. What appeared to be the final chapter for the Scafidi house came when the bracing winds and tidal rush of Hurricane Katrina in 2005 ruined walls, destroyed roof, and warped floors, until the theater, which lost its playhouse in the storm, came in and rescued the dilapidated home. According to BSLLT Board President Cheryl Grace, "We could have had a steel building up within a year and started productions. But the Board made the decision to find a still-standing building in the community and restore it. This was definitely the harder path to go, but our community lost so much that we thought if we could save just one building from being razed because of Katrina damage, we would be doing our part for the struggling community." A grant from the Mississippi Arts Commission, combined with private donations and memberships, helped to restore the building to its former glory and solidify a new home for theater in Hancock County.

According to Grace, this restoration was a critical part of renewing downtown. She says, "We saved one of the few remaining buildings in our community. We took a ma and pa grocery store from the 1920s and breathed new, creative life into it. I bet Mr. Scafidi could never have imagined what his original sweat and effort was going to be adapted to do. We felt if the community could see this project emerge, see an abandoned building get new life after Katrina, see the human effort go into it, it would certainly provide inspiration for the renewal of each of their lives. Theater inspires, connects, energizes. Theater matters."

Today, the BSLLT holds performances throughout the year and draws participation ranging from retirees seeking community involvement to youngsters partaking in summer programs in order to learn the rudiments of stage acting. The theater is, by all accounts, serving as one of the anchors of downtown Bay St. Louis.

The same element of rebirth is happening right now in other cities across Mississippi. From the Ellis Theater in Cleveland to the Riley Center in Meridian, the state is filled with fine examples of how restoration enhances the social and cultural life of locals while providing high quality venues to be enjoyed by tourists and visitors.

One of the heroes of this type of restoration is the Mississippi Arts Commission, which funds many projects designed to save beautiful old structures. According to Executive Director Malcolm White, "We love rehabbing old buildings. This program has saved many historic buildings from the wrecking ball and turned them into performing and arts centers. All Mississippians deserve access to the arts, whether they live in a community of 500 people or of 5,000 people. Our goal is to provide an 'address' for the arts in every community.

"What's really, *really* powerful is when there is a performance, but there is also a class connected with it, or a Q&A following it… we are always looking for a way to engage young people." White adds, however, that it really is about encouraging the entire creative class, which may include everything from children to empty nesters and retirees.

Another theater supported by the Mississippi Arts Commission is in the Mary C. O'Keefe Cultural Center of Arts and Education in Ocean Springs, which provides performance space for music, theater, and comedy performances, as well as gallery space for visual artists. The main thrust of what the "Mary C." provides -- arts education for adults as well as children -- is exactly the kind of focus Malcolm White was praising. Listed on the National Register of Historic Places, the building housing this critical resource was built in 1927 as a public school building. In 1999 it became the Mary C. O'Keefe Cultural Center, and many major restorations to the property have happened since that time.

Another example of a historic "rescue" on the coast is the Saenger Theater in Biloxi, which underwent an extensive renovation in 1999, an anchor for the revitalization of the creative vibe of downtown Biloxi. Now there is an ever growing selection of art galleries and museums in downtown Biloxi, with some housed in historic structures themselves. Built in 1929, the theater hosted some of the earliest talkie films of cinema and provided a stage for vaudeville acts and traveling shows. The beautiful sign on the theater exterior is an iconic image for people of the Gulf Coast, attesting to the importance of keeping such architectural treasures alive. For people of the coast, who lost so much during Hurricane Katrina, structures such as the Saenger and the Bay St. Louis Little Theater tell the story of South Mississippi.

Larry Morrisey, who works with the Building Fund for the Arts Projects of the Mississippi Arts Commission, believes in the value of restoring old venues for new purposes. "Historic downtown theaters were important gathering points in small-town Mississippi for much of the 20th century," he said. "While it's not feasible for most of them to still show movies, we've seen in numerous towns how old theaters have been transformed into arts centers that serve multiple uses for the community."

Mississippian native playwright, Tennessee Williams, loved to represent the South in all of its elegant, yet crumbling, glory. The story of the Bay St. Louis Little Theater is coincidentally similar to the house depicted in the expanded film version of this play set in rural Mississippi. In a way, many historic buildings of the coast, particularly those that survived Katrina, bear scars similar to those of the Starr Boarding house, which was a fictional victim of a changing economy. Although the downtowns of Mississippi have increasingly changed in response to economic realities, one thing is always the same: by keeping the architectural past alive, preservationists help the state's cultural and creative future to unfurl.

Parts of this article originally appeared in
Mississippi Legends Magazine.

Bay St. Louis Theater:
398 Blaize Avenue, Bay St. Louis, Ms 39520
Phone: 228-864-2882
Website: http://www.bsllt.org

Biloxi Saenger Theater:
170 Reynoir Street, Biloxi, MS

Mary C. O'Keefe Cultural Center of Arts and Education
1600 Government Street, Ocean Springs, MS 39564
Phone: 228-818-2878
Website: http://www.maryc.org

Gulf Coast Symphony Orchestra

Deanna Vogt – Long Beach, MS
Photos by Leo Ridge III, www.ridgeimage.com

The orchestra tunes up. The lights go down. Stage light reflects off the focused faces of the musicians and their instruments. A first refrain develops. The audience settles into the sound and story, enveloped in the joy of performance, watching people do together something they love so well and could not do alone.

Based in Biloxi but representing the Mississippi Gulf Coast region, the Gulf Coast Symphony Orchestra has provided over fifty years of classical and popular symphony music to the community. Founded in 1962 by Dr. James Graves with an orchestra of thirty-five musicians, over the next three decades it grew to the present size of seventy. These decades have seen much growth and change in the orchestra, currently under the direction of the innovative and determined Dr. John Strickler as the fifth conductor.

The Gulf Coast Symphony Orchestra is a regional orchestra, drawing professional musicians from throughout the northern Gulf Coast, including Baton Rouge, Mobile, Pensacola, and throughout Mississippi. The orchestra generally presents seven scheduled concerts each year, September through May, many of them featuring guest performers. Beyond the main musical season of classical performances, the season includes a pops concert, featuring music from non-classical genres like musicals, movie soundtracks, jazz, or other popular categories; Memorial Day weekend concerts; and the very popular Holiday Peppermint Pops, which occurs on the weekend of the Thanksgiving holiday. Of these, perhaps the most popular are the two annual outdoor Memorial Day concerts, *Sounds by the Sea*. These seaside concert weekends, instigated by Dr.

Strickler to bring orchestra music to the general public, draw over 10,000 attendees. The Memorial Day concerts are free and include a family-friendly musical tribute, great views, evening fireworks, and a sea of celebrants relaxing in lawn chairs and on picnic blankets.

Special performances inserted into the concert season have included benefit concerts featuring headlining popular performers. One of the most memorable concerts since Dr. Strickler arrived was a concert with Luciano Pavarotti (one of the most beloved tenors in history), an event enjoyed by 11,000 people. The orchestra's performance was so successful that they received an offer to tour with Andrea Bocelli, another globally popular Italian tenor.

In addition to concerts, the Gulf Coast Symphony Orchestra offers a wide range of experiences to enhance the enjoyment of the music, support music awareness and the availability of a professional orchestra in the community, and enhance the pleasure of other activities on the Mississippi Gulf Coast. During the concert season the public can enjoy an up-close experience with the conductor and featured performer by attending Maestro Strickler's *Words on Music*. A free-to-the-public *Words on Music* is typically held at the Walter Anderson Museum of Art in Ocean Springs on Thursday evenings before the concert weekend, and at the Great Southern Club in Gulfport's Hancock Building at lunchtime on Friday with a luncheon fee. *Words on Music* events are an informal discussion about the upcoming concert, with personal perspectives on the music from the conductor and guest artist. The public should check the symphony's website to verify the schedule and location of *Words on Music*, as they may vary from season to season.

Through a program called *Finishing Touches*, the orchestra offers the opportunity to attend the late afternoon dress rehearsals prior to each scheduled Saturday night classical concert. With a reduced price ticket, anyone can enjoy being in the audience as the music receives its finishing touches before the evening performance.

Special fundraising events are another source of enjoyment beyond the music. The most popular of these is the annual *Barbecue under the Oaks*, a springtime celebration more than twenty-five years old, held the last Saturday of March on Don and Peggy Spraberry's homestead on Menge Avenue in Pass Christian. Featuring over twenty-five regional chefs and restaurants offering ribs, sausages, oysters, desserts, and other foods, the event attracts a great turnout. For the price of the admission ticket, every participant chooses as much food as they like while enjoying musical entertainment from the Youth Orchestra.

Other popular events organized by the orchestra's Guild include home tours, food tastings, teas, tablescapes, and an autumn golf tournament called *Strokes for Notes*. From year to year other creative offerings have provided entertainment for the community. *Dinner with a Tenor* offers a gourmet meal in a beautiful setting, with a visiting guest performer providing entertainment and insightful conversation.

Another example of creative fundraising embraced by the community is a set of playing card decks featuring landmarks of the Mississippi Gulf Coast. The card decks, produced by the Guild, are available at the orchestra's office and special sales events. Featuring a special landmark of the Coast on each card, contributors purchased the right to select the feature for each card in the deck through local store displays. This highly successful fundraiser won an award from a national league of orchestra guilds, as did *Barbecue Under the Oaks*.

Long time Guild member and leader Betty Oswald explains that the Orchestra Guild is a citizen's organization associated as a support association for the symphony. Ticket sales account for a very small percentage of the total income required to keep a professional orchestra running. In addition to corporate and private contributions and grants, the orchestra depends on the fundraising efforts of the Guild. The Gulf Coast Symphony Orchestra Guild has been in place since 1965, and counts around 100 members who take responsibility for this economic and artistic mission.

The orchestra continually works toward new initiatives for community engagement. Dr. Strickler is exploring a music wellness program with ties to music therapy. Such programs involve going to assisted living, hospital settings, neonatal units, and cancer wards. The idea is to have musicians go into care facilities or retirement communities, working with the medical community for the benefit of community members with a variety of care needs.

Every successful classical orchestra works to stay relevant in contemporary culture. With the head-snapping pace of cultural change today, innovative approaches to reaching new, diverse and younger audiences is a national trend. Dr. Strickler conducts the Gulf Coast Symphony Youth Orchestra, established in 2001, as an educational program under the umbrella of the main symphony.

This is an honors orchestra drawing from public and private schools, as well as home-schooled students in the area. The Youth Orchestra provides school day concerts each season and is involved in other educational outreach events, for example, performing at a charity walk-a-thon. From nourishing the Youth Orchestra and bringing kid-friendly music appreciation to school children, to providing special programs or price reductions for students, young adults and military personnel, and outreach to infirm or elderly adults, the orchestra wants to improve its service to the larger community wherever possible.

Since 2009 the Gulf Coast Symphony Orchestra has been part of the national *Link Up* program organized by the Weill Institute of Carnegie Hall. This is a yearlong music curriculum designed to teach rhythm and melody, critical listening, and music reading, and involve students in composition and improvisation. Several area schools send hundreds of elementary students to join the Youth Orchestra in an end-of-the-year concert at the Biloxi Saenger Theater. Students join in the music making from the audience. Each student receives a small plastic instrument they use to play along with the Youth Orchestra as the accompanying presentation shows them when to play. The program features recognizable tunes, many of them based on classical music melodies.

Audience engagement is just as critical for the main concert series of the Gulf Coast Symphony Orchestra. Dr. Strickler is often praised for his innovative concert programs where he blends the familiar and progressive. "Making it fun is important," Dr. Strickler says. "Innovation in programming is an essential way to introduce surprising elements, to delight audiences with the unexpected, and to keep a classic musical form fresh for contemporary audiences." The overture, concerto, and grand symphony may appear in a non-traditional order on the program. "While planning," Dr. Strickler says, he seeks to "Mix things up, pair things, like planning a menu. What are we doing as a first course? Maybe put the salad at the end as they do in Europe.

"It's important to find pieces that are listener friendly, especially if the composer is not well known." Dr. Strickler continually looks for new pieces that have broad appeal, particularly for a younger audience. "People want to hear what's happening now," he says. He likes to include pieces by living composers. "I liken it to an art gallery with changing exhibits, old things and new things as opposed to a museum where all you see is old stuff. Even museums, the good ones, are learning to not just show all the old stuff, but to have changing exhibits."

Dr. Strickler also likes to relate the music and the orchestra to the audience in a more personal way. "I generally speak from the stage – it's part of making a connection." In a performance that fell on Halloween weekend, the conductor emerged onstage from a coffin-like box, then turned to greet the delighted audience in full Dracula makeup, a long cape falling back over his tuxedo. He conducted the entire orchestra program in his spooky regalia.

Dr. Strickler selects featured artists from around the country. He may work through artist representatives, or call on musicians he has worked with through the years. Others may contact him with recorded samples of their work and negotiate arrangements for a potential appearance. One concert program came from a Kansas composer who had written a concerto for the principal trombonist of the New York Philharmonic. When Dr. Strickler left Topeka, where he was conducting the Topeka Symphony Orchestera in addition to his work with the Gulf Coast Symphony Orchestra, the composer was delighted for the piece to premiere on the Mississippi Gulf Coast, so the New York Philharmonic trombonist arranged to play this featured piece in Mississippi.

Dr. Strickler works with program themes that allow the pieces, composers, and featured musicians or instruments to tell a cohesive story. One such concert featured a Native American flute player with concertos for Native American flute. The conductor tied in the theme by adding Dvorak's *New World Symphony*. First performed in 1893, Dvorak was inspired in this composition by Native American music, story, and celebration.

The strength of an organization is shown in its ability to continue through adversity. In September of 2001, Dr. Strickler was commuting to the Mississippi Coast from Topeka, Kansas. Strickler had led two rehearsals on the Coast on Sunday, September 9, 2001, before returning to Topeka, expecting to return on Thursday, September 13 to finish preparations for the Saturday concert. With the 9/11 attacks, the government halted all civilian air traffic, implementing for the first time its thirty-year-old emergency preparedness plan for air traffic security control. Dr. Strickler barely made it back to the Coast in time, and the scheduled soloist was unable to get here at all. Nevertheless, the orchestra opened the evening concert on

Saturday, September 15, with a special tribute to those who lost their lives on that grave day, not yet a week old in history. The memorial selection was American composer Samuel Barber's *Adagio for Strings*, a famously tender and elegant piece composed in the depths of the nation's Great Depression and on the precipice of a second world war. Opening the post-9/11 concert on the Coast with this historic piece, Dr. Strickler first asked the audience to hold applause for the special tribute. However, the music and the moment struck the audience powerfully. After a moment of silence following the *Adagio for Strings*, the orchestra launched into the national anthem, which traditionally opens their concerts.

"The audience shot out of their seats. They sang their hearts out. I have never been so moved by the national anthem," remembers Dr. Strickler. The orchestra's performance that concert night provided an opportunity for a stunned community to come together in the aftermath of astonishing tragedy and be comforted through the powerful expression and solace of fine music.

In August 2005 Hurricane Katrina devastated the Gulf Coast, including destroying most of the infrastructure. The orchestra's performance home, the historic Biloxi Saenger Theater, was extensively damaged, including much of the roof, resulting in massive interior water damage. Determined to continue their season, a local school auditorium became the orchestra's home away from home during repairs to the Saenger.

"We did get an orchestra back together," Dr. Strickler said. "The audience was so appreciative. We needed something to get our minds off the ugliness around us. Relief is the word for it, a respite, a chance to think about something else."

There are many popular misconceptions about symphony music, such as the belief that you have to have a degree in music to appreciate it. "Actually," Dr. Strickler says, "while it doesn't hurt if you have a music background, you can enjoy it without knowing a thing about musical structure. Also, we don't care what you wear." Some attendees wear dressy or sometimes even formal wear, while others wear basic pieces of nice casual clothing.

Another common anxiety about attending a classical music concert is knowing when to clap. Dr. Strickler advises, "If you're moved to applaud, do so. Seventy musicians want to know you appreciate what they're doing." It used to be that you did not applaud between movements in the piece being performed. Today, the philosophy is, "If you're moved to applaud, applaud."

Come enjoy music on the Gulf Coast at the Biloxi Saenger Theater during the regular season, or at one of the many special concerts or events. The professional magnificence will be the highlight of your visit, and no one will care what you wear.

Gulf Coast Symphony Orchestra offices
11975 Seaway Road, Suite A130, Gulfport, MS 39503
Phone: (228) 896-4276
Website: http://www.gulfcoastsymphony.net
For news and connection, also find the
Gulf Coast Symphony Orchestra on Facebook:
https://www.facebook.com/Gulf-Coast-Symphony/149900182846

Biloxi Saenger Theater
170 Reynoir Street, Biloxi, MS 39530
Phone: (228) 435-6291

Fishing on the Mississippi Gulf Coast

Keith Goodfellow, MD – Gulfport, MS

Opportunities for the fishing enthusiast are almost limitless on the Mississippi Gulf Coast. Fishing is a year-round attraction that can be enjoyed on any budget. One can experience fresh water fishing on the coastal rivers, brackish water fishing in the bays, saltwater fishing on the beaches and sound, or blue water fishing in the Gulf of Mexico. An angler can walk onto a public fishing pier or beach, fish out of his own boat, or hire a local captain and charter boat.

Successful fresh water fishing for largemouth bass, pan fish, catfish, and striped bass can be accomplished all year on the coastal rivers, but peaks in late winter and spring. In the fall, saltwater pushes up the mouths of these rivers bringing saltwater species of fish. November is prime time for slow trolling for speckled trout. The Pearl and Pascagoula River systems are the largest and are well known for bass fishing. They also are home to the endangered Gulf sturgeon, which should be released if caught. The Jourdan and Wolf rivers empty into the Bay of St. Louis, while the Tchoutacabouffe and Biloxi rivers empty into Biloxi Bay.

The Bay of St. Louis and Biloxi Bay offer exceptional small boat angling. During the winter and early spring red drum (locally known as redfish), black drum, and sheepshead can be found near the bridges that cross the bays. They can be fooled into biting by fishing on the bottom with cracked crab or dead shrimp. Be ready, as many of these drum weigh over thirty pounds. Late spring, summer, and fall, speckled trout and white trout invade the bays. The trout can be found at the bridges, over artificial reefs, and under flocks of seagulls feeding on shrimp. Bottom fishing for these trout at the bridges and artificial reefs can be productive, but often fishing bait under a popping cork can be more successful. Live shrimp, which can be purchased at one of the local bait shops, is almost perfect bait for these trout. Artificial lures and dead shrimp can also be used with success. If you can catch live menhaden (locally known as pogey) in a cast net, they make fantastic bait for trout. It is not unusual to catch an ice chest full of white trout using this bait in the fall while fishing at one of the bridges. Mississippi has no size or number limit on these great tasting white trout. During the summer and fall, redfish and flounder can be caught along the grassy or sandy shorelines using a variety of natural or artificial baits.

A number of public access fishing piers exist in the three coastal counties and most are free of charge. They are on the bays and front beaches. Being well lighted, they are particularly popular to locals who enjoy night fishing during the summer. This is a great way to beat the heat and experience some of the local color. The lights attract baitfish and shrimp, which in turn attract larger fish. During the summer and early fall a mixed assortment of fish can be caught here. It would not be unusual in the same night to catch croaker, whiting (locally known as ground mullet), white trout, speckled trout, redfish, flounder, black drum, sheepshead, and shark. Large jack crevalles frequent the front beach piers of Harrison County in the summer and early fall. Many an unprepared angler has had all the line stripped off his reel by one of these brutes.

Wade fishing off the front beaches is productive from spring through fall. It is best when there has been little or no rain over the prior few days. This allows for higher salinities and clearer water. The main quarry for the wade fisherman is speckled trout, and secondarily, flounder or red drum. Peak fishing time is from dawn until about 9 a.m. This allows plenty of time to enjoy other Gulf Coast attractions. Live shrimp is the best bait for this type of fishing. For those fishermen who prefer artificial lures, hard and soft plastic baits as well as the tried and true silver spoon work well.

On calm nights eerie appearing lights often appear over the shallow waters just off the beach. These are not UFO's, but the lights of fishermen looking for flounder. A variety of lights and spears can be purchased at local tackle shops to participate in this endeavor. The lights are used to visualize the outline of the flounder on the sand bottom. The flounder is then stuck with a spear to capture it. Silence is important so as to not scare away the flounder before it is seen. The best nights are when there is a calm wind and the moon is obscured by clouds or prior to moonrise. The best tidal condition is at the beginning of a rising tide. These lights can be seen along the beaches spring through fall, but flounder are particularly abundant in September and October.

The Mississippi Department of Marine Resources (DMR) has constructed a series of crushed limestone reefs marked by white PVC pipes and signs just off the beaches in approximately six feet of water. The GPS coordinates for all the DMR reefs can be obtained from the Mississippi Department of Marine Resources website (www.dmr.state.ms.us). These near-shore reefs can be reached with small boats or kayaks. In late winter through spring they will begin attracting ground mullet and black drum. As the water continues to warm they will attract white trout and speckled trout in the summer and fall. Ground mullet and drum can be caught bottom fishing with dead shrimp or crab as bait. White trout can also be caught by fishing on the bottom with dead shrimp, but speckled trout are more likely to be caught with live shrimp under a popping cork. During summer the trout tend to feed most actively at dawn and dusk. White trout usually are caught right over the reef, but the speckled trout tend to be in the deeper water just over the edge of the reef.

The DMR has also constructed reefs of rubble from demolished buildings and bridges. These are in the Mississippi Sound within a few miles of shore. These reefs extend above the surface of the water and can provide boaters protection from wind and waves. Jailhouse Reef and Square Handkerchief Reef (also known as Gene Taylor Reef) are in Hancock County. Pass Christian and Katrina Reefs are in Harrison County. All the usual inshore species of saltwater fish common to this area can be caught at these reefs, but these reefs are increasingly becoming known for trophy speckled trout. The fishermen targeting these large speckled trout prefer live croaker or finger mullet for bait. When these baits are not available, hard plastic top water or slow sinking lures, as well as soft plastic swim baits are used. Live shrimp can be used to catch larger numbers of school size speckled trout and white trout. Live bait should be fished anywhere water flows through or around the structure. Top water lures should be fished right next to the structure.

Several low profile crushed limestone reefs have been created by the DMR farther out in the Mississippi Sound closer to the barrier islands. These are known to produce white trout, ground mullet, and sheepshead. During the summer they can become overrun by Atlantic sharpnose sharks, which can be caught on almost any type of natural bait.

Natural reefs also can be found in the Mississippi Sound. Two of the most popular are marked by the skeletal remains of old lighthouses. Pass Marianne light sits south of Pass Christian and marks a large oyster reef. Weather permitting, from early spring to late fall there is almost always at least one boat fishing here. This location at times is packed with fishing boats. Please be courteous toward the other fishermen. Due to the strong current and thick oyster shells, anchoring can be difficult. Be prepared with a long anchor line or two anchors. Fish can be caught here on natural or artificial bait. Speckled trout are generally the targeted species here and can be found anywhere in the water column. A slip float rig often makes finding the best depth easier. At the western tip of Cat Island sits "The Birdcage." It marks the edge of a sand flat two to four feet deep that abruptly drops to approximately ten feet deep. Speckled trout and redfish can be caught on the flat, but the better fishing may be at the drop off in deeper water. Fishing with live bait on the bottom has produced some monster trout.

Late spring through fall, trolling in the Mississippi Sound can produce redfish, Spanish mackerel, sharks and jack crevalles. Several size spoons or feather dusters can be pulled. Weighted lines or using planers allows for fishing different depths in the water column.

Cat Island, Ship Island, Horn Island and Petit Bois Island are Mississippi's barrier islands. During the winter large schools of bull reds and black drum can be seen and sight fished over the shallow clear waters of the sand flats. Sheepshead also tend to congregate around any structure near the islands during February. During the warmer months, speckled trout can be found in the grass beds on the north sides of the islands or in the surf on the south sides. The bull reds will be found in the surf or in the passes. Pompano are a summer visitor to the islands. They can be caught on the shallow sand flats by using a small hook with a piece of dead shrimp and a colored bead above the hook. Another summer visitor, large and small sharks can be found anywhere around the islands. During their spring migration in late April and May, cobia can be caught over the sandbars using a chumming technique. During their fall migration in September and October, they are found near channel markers and can be sight fished. Tripletail are another fish which are attracted to channel markers or any floating object and can be sight fished during the summer and early fall. They are most likely to be hooked using a live shrimp under a float.

Beyond the barrier islands trolling produces king mackerel, Spanish mackerel, redfish, jack crevalles, and shark. The DMR has constructed a series of offshore reefs in which large objects such as ships, barges, and concrete balls sit on the bottom. These reefs produce sheepshead, black drum, redfish, snapper, shark, and an occasional grouper. Oil rigs dot the surface of the Gulf of Mexico beyond the DMR reefs. These manmade structures support ecosystems as diverse as any Caribbean reef. Red snapper, mangrove snapper, amberjack and grouper are just a few of the species these oil rigs attract.

The "Thousand Fathom Curve" in the Gulf of Mexico is the realm of the serious blue water fisherman. Yellowfin tuna and wahoo can be caught throughout the year, but are the main catch during the winter. As the water warms and the Loop Current gets closer to the mouth of the Mississippi River, marlin and mahi-mahi become more abundant.

Public fishing contests are frequent here, especially during the summer. The Mississippi Gulf Coast Billfish Classic in early June features the blue marlin, but also awards prizes for other blue water species. This contest draws some of the largest and most beautiful sport fishing boats in the northern Gulf of Mexico to compete out of Biloxi, Mississippi. In 2013 over a million dollars in prizes were awarded to the fifty-two registered boats. The Mississippi Deep Sea Fishing Rodeo awards prizes for many saltwater species as well as freshwater. Registration for the Mississippi Deep Sea Fishing Rodeo is free. This contest has traditionally been held during the July fourth holiday.

Plenty of opportunities exist on the Mississippi Gulf Coast for one to enjoy fishing from shore or on one's own boat, but the experience may be enhanced by hiring a local charter captain. One can be contacted through the Mississippi Charter Boat Captains Association (mscharterboats.org). Fishing licenses can be purchased at local sporting goods stores, by telephone (1-800-546-4868), or online (mdwfp.com).

Bird Watching on the Mississippi Coast

W. Michiel Hawkins, PhD – Gautier, MS

The summer sun heats an area of moist ground in a small pine savannah creating an invisible bubble of warm air. This becomes a thermal bubble that rises in a doughnut shape skyward. As the thermal rises a Swallow-tailed kite lifts with the invisible elevator to seek insects. Each sweeping turn of the bird displays a white underside giving the bird a very distinctive shape. The kite continues over open savannahs until it hits a woodland bordering a marsh, there finding winged insects as it wanders over a great range of coastal territory. This is only one of many unique birds to be observed on the Mississippi Gulf Coast.

The Mississippi coastal habitat provides avid bird watchers with over three hundred and eight-seven species to record on their life-list. This means nearly all orders of birds in a standard field guide may be found in this area.

In fall, winter, and early spring, on a boat ride to Ship or Horn Island, often a single Lone Common Loon may be seen or heard. Rarely do you find this bird on land. It may be heard near to shore on late evening or early morning.

Grebes are another group of northern visitors spending much of the winter in Gulf Coastal waters. Horned Grebes in flocks or individuals can be seen feeding in marsh ponds, bayous attaching to the Gulf. Look for the white face and neck and the tufts on the head representing its namesake. Very shy, but ever present in shallow fresh-water ponds are the Pied-Billed and Least Grebe. With a good pair of field glasses on a dock or the edge of the pond you can watch them dive and bob-up ever watchful of your behavior.

Skipping several deep Ocean Orders in the field guides move to the Pelicans. Once rare and endangered, the pelican is now again common on the coast. Both the Brown and American White Pelican are common on beaches and piers. The Brown Pelican provides great photographic subjects in flight and fishing. They will fly in long lines gliding and following a leader that may skim the water and then rise with a quick flapping of wings and settle back into a glide. The dive after fish looks like a control crash followed by a fast takeoff and back to flight. On some piers you may be greeted by a pelican begging for food. Be careful! The bill can hurt a hand and scratch a camera lens.

American White pelicans are winter visitors. They fly in a V-formation and fish quite differently from the Brown pelicans. They come from large freshwater lakes north of the Coast. A breeding colony lives at the Ross Barnett Reservoir north of Jackson, MS.

Magnificent Frigate birds may be observed off the island and over the sound in rough weather and times of severe storm. They wander about the Gulf and are very beautiful and graceful in flight. In late August through early September the author observed five flying and soaring off the east end of Deer Island. After about fifteen minutes of soaring to altitude the small flock set a course south toward deeper Gulf. Another wanderer is the Gannet. Look for them to be resting out on spits of sand and in flocks of other birds on the islands. Use of a spotting scope may be best for the resting bird. Look for them also in flight during threatening weather.

Of the Cormorant and Anhinga order, two are common along the coast: the Double-Crested Cormorant and the Anhinga. The Double-crested Cormorant can be seen on abandoned pilings after they have done a morning's fishing. They fly single file over the water going to roost or to feed.

The Anhinga occurs in fresh water lakes, swamps and ponds. They swim with their body submerged and have to climb up and sun to dry their wings before flight. Their appearance while swimming has gained them the nickname Snakebird for the long slender neck that is out of the water as they swim.

Coastal waterfowl include geese, surface feeding ducks, an uncommon Tree Duck, Bay ducks, Sea ducks, Stiff tails, and, of course, Mergansers. The coast can boast the Canada Goose as a year around inhabitant as well as a winter visitor. Common around fresh water lakes and golf watercourses they can become pests. In winter, White-Fronted, Blues, and Snow geese may be seen.

A favorite to find, usually in flocks, are the surface-feeding ducks. Mallards are common during winter in brackish water, bayous and freshwater lakes. Black ducks can be seen in coastal waters, marshes and bayous. They, like the Mottled Duck, use marshes in common with Mallard, Pintails, Gadwalls and American Widgeon. They are reported at the mouth of the Pearl and Pascagoula rivers in winter. In early September it is not unusual to see Blue-Winged and Green-Winged teals in ponds and lakes north of the Coast.

The prize of all the ducks to photograph is the male Wood Duck. Over the last fifty years this duck has made a great comeback over all Mississippi. River systems emptying into the Gulf, bayous, and small ponds now host this bird in good numbers. Be patient if this is a birding goal and you will be rewarded. It has been stated that in spring the male possesses eighteen different colors.

Although Tree ducks are not common species in Mississippi, with protection and habitat they've become coastal residents. Observed species include the Fulvous Tree Duck and Whistling Tree Duck reported near Bay St. Louis.

Bay ducks are best observed from a boat, from the beach or shore, with a spotting scope needed for identification. When you do see them you immediately know why their group is defined as a raft. Look for Redheads, Canvas Backs, Ring-Necked ducks, Greater and Lesser Scaup, Common Golden Eye and the colorful Bufflehead. Bays, inlets and the open Gulf may be the haunt of this order.

Stiff-Tailed ducks, such as the Ruddy Duck, may be found in some estuaries, lakes or rivers. Look for the white cheek patches and the tail feathers that are vertical when this duck is swimming. The Hooded Merganser is the most often reported of the order of fish-eating diving ducks. It is common in winter in estuaries.

Of the order of vultures, hawks and falcons, both species of vultures, are found soaring or roadside having a meal. Black and Turkey vultures can be seen in flocks and as single individuals. The Mississippi Coastal resident Swallow-Tailed Kite may be observed soaring over city or a rural area.

Ospreys are plentiful along bayous connected to the Gulf. They nest in large cypress or other trees near the open water or marsh. Expect to see them flying and diving for fish early morning or late afternoon. Watch how skillful they fly with fish, always pointing the fish's head in the direction of flight. A good many nest sites are currently on the south side of Deer Island.

The American Bald Eagle is making a comeback on both the Pascagoula and Pearl River basins. There are more nest sites being reported each year and more birds observed. It is not uncommon to see them flying over neighborhoods and down the coastline. Nest sites include, but are not limited to, the Pascagoula and Pearl River basins. Herons and wading birds are extremely plentiful on the coast. The habitat serves them well and the variety of species is strong in number. They may be seen in road ditches, lakes, streams, coastline and sometimes in backyards fishing in goldfish ponds. Great White Herons, Common Egrets, Snowy Egrets (with bright yellow feet), Cattle Egrets originally from Africa, Little Blue Herons, Great Blue Heron, Louisiana Heron and Green Heron can be seen around boat launches, road ditches, lakes and on the beach. Black-Crowned and Yellow-Crowned Night herons along with American and Least Bitterns may be found hunting in marsh areas.

Special mention needs to be made for a birder to insure they attempt to observe the Mississippi Sandhill Crane. There is a Sandhill Crane Refuge for these birds north of the town of Gautier easily accessible from Highway 90 or Interstate-10. In winter there are tours to see the area and a walking track where other birds may be observed. You might see a pair of these birds on farms north of the refuge or on golf courses. If you see them on the roadside please use extreme caution in passing.

The small Sora Rail can be found along marsh edges. In my experience they are a happy accident to see. Size and coloration let them hide easily. Clapper Rails, common in the marsh, are resident birds that are easily heard but not seen. They will communicate across the marsh with one bird starting the call and then the next, and then the next, like a wave of calls. As quickly as the calling starts it quits. Yellow and Black rails have been reported as rare sightings.

There are other orders to report, though space does not allow a covering of all species living in this area, such as sparrows, warblers, mockingbirds, Blue Jays, blue birds, robins and crows all are residents. Your favorite bird may be missing from this article. Some years migrating birds over-fly the coast in spring, some years they stop. Migrants appear all over the coast, but some stopover areas are the Pearl River and Pascagoula Basins. The below listed areas host more birds than aforementioned. These are not all the birding sites on the coast. You may step out the door of your lodging and begin seeing birds. It has often been said that you are never more than fifty-feet from a bird - and that is certainly true of the Mississippi Gulf Coast.

Places to Visit:
Grand Bay National Estuarine Research Reserve and Vicinity
6005 Bayou Heron Road, Moss Point, MS - 39562
Phone: 228-475-7047
Office Hours: Monday-Friday 7:30 a.m. – 4 p.m.
Interpretative area: Monday- Friday 9 a.m. – 3 p.m.

Mississippi Sandhill Crane
National Wildlife Refuge
7200 Crane lane, Gautier, MS - 39553
228-497-6322
Open Tuesday- Saturday, 9 a.m. -3p.m

Gulf Islands National Sea Shore
Davis Bayou Area, 3500 Park Road, Ocean Springs, MS - 39564
228-875-9057

Ship Island Excursions
Gulfport Yacht Harbor, Gulfport, MS
Phone 228-864-1014

Shepard State Park
1034 Graveline Drive, Gautier, MS - 39553
228-497-2244

Buccaneer State Park
1150 South Beach Boulevard -Waveland, MS - 39576
Phone 228-467-3822

Photo Credits

Pensacola Beach	Two photos of Beach: Melissa Carrigee
Dauphin Island	Pier, Ft. Gaines: Jeff D. Johnston
Walking the T	Two photos of Ocean Springs: Fowler McLain
Welcome to Biloxi	Biloxi Lighthouse, Biloxi Visitors' Center: Philip L. Levin
Traveling the Coast Road	Two photos off of Hwy 90: Sue Monkress
Henderson Point	Bridge detail, Point view: Stanley Hastings
Gulf Islands National Seashore	Two photos of the Seashore: Sherryl LaPointe
Bellingrath Gardens	Photos courtesy of Bellingrath Gardens and Home
Round Island Lighthouse	Lighthouse pre-Katrina : Marcia Baumhauer Lighthouse under reconstruction: Brenda Finnegan
Pascagoula River Audubon Center	Two photos from site: Philip L. Levin
Good Karma Café	Two photos from restaurant: Cecily Cummings
Mary Mahoney's Old French House	Two photos from restaurant: Philip L. Levin
Old Biloxi Cemetery	Two photos from cemetery: Jason Taylor
Dusti Bongé Museum	Photo of museum: Cecily Cummings Photo of art work: Billy Dugger
Sie's Place	Two photos: Courtesy of family of Sie Simon
Lynn Meadows Discovery Center	Two photos of center: Philip L. Levin
IMMS	Two photos of CMER: Abby Livengood Chatelain
Beauvoir	Photo of Beauvoir building: Anne McKee Photo of graveyard: Philip L. Levin
Ohr O'Keefe	Two Photos of museum: Denny Mecham
Friendship Oak	Two photos of tree: Jamie O'Quinn
Infinity Space Center	Two photos of center: Ellis Anderson
Gulf Coast Theaters	Two photos of theaters: Philip L. Levin
Gulf Coast Symphony	Photos of symphony: Courtesy of *The Sun Herald* and Leo J. Ridge III
Fishing on the MS Coast	Two photos of fishing: Keith Goodfellow
Bird Watching	Black Skimmers, Ospreys, Blue Heron: Philip L. Levin

Author Bios

Ellis Anderson's first book, *Under Surge, Under Siege,* was published by University Press of Mississippi in 2010 and has garnered several awards, including the Eudora Welty 2010 Book Prize and the 2011 Mississippi Library Association's Author Award. In 2012, it was one of a dozen books shortlisted for Stanford University's International Saroyan Prize for non-fiction. Anderson's articles, essays and photographs have appeared in numerous publications, including *MSNBC*, *Salon,* and *Southern Cultures*. She divides time between Bay St. Louis, Mississippi and New Orleans, working full-time as a freelance writer, photographer and media consultant.

Freelance writer and editor **Kara Martinez Bachman** has read her work for national broadcast on *NPR (National Public Radio)*. Her creative nonfiction has appeared in *The Writer*, one of the oldest and most respected magazines in the nation. Kara is a freelance newspaper columnist for the New Orleans *Times-Picayune* Northshore Bureau and *nola.com.* She is Managing Editor for *Parents & Kids-Gulf Coast* and *Parents & Kids-Pine Belt,* and is a regular contributor to *Legends: Culture and Arts from the Cradle of American Music.* Her writing has appeared in numerous publications and literary journals, including *American Fitness, VIVMag, Mississippi Magazine, San Diego Family, Mississippi Weddings, Birmingham Parent* and *The Independent.*

Melissa Carrigee fell in love with the written word at a young age and began writing poetry and short stories for school contests. Since then she has written numerous articles for Parents and Kids magazine and authored *"Adventures in Home Building: Written From a Woman's Point of View"*. By profession she is an early childhood educator that holds a Business, Web Design and Graphic Design degree, which offers her the opportunity to expend her other creative talents. Through her web-based business, Carrigee Design Consulting, Melissa creates web pages for businesses and personal use. Melissa lived in Pensacola, Florida for fourteen years before meeting her husband in 2001. The couple, and their two sons, reside on the Mississippi Gulf Coast close enough to make Pensacola a regular get away destination for the family.

Lauren Clark is the author of three novels, including *Dancing Naked in Dixie* and *Stardust Summer*. She is a member of the Gulf Coast Writers Association, the Mobile Writers Guild, and a regular contributor to *Parents & Kids* Magazine's Mississippi Gulf Coast Edition. Check out her website at www.laurenclarkbooks.com.

John Cuevas served as creative director of his own advertising and design firm in Atlanta for over 25 years. Before starting his company, he had worked for several major advertising agencies. During his career he won gold awards in radio, television, and print advertising. He has been researching the history of Cat Island for over fifty years, and has gathered the most complete set of archival documents. He has written articles and lectured on the subject, and his book, *Cat Island: The History of a Mississippi Gulf Coast Barrier Island* (McFarland, 2011), is the first documented history of the island.

Cecily Cummings is a native of Gulfport, MS, but spent much of her childhood living in Europe. This early exposure to the creative culture inspired her to become a writer and artist.

She is currently a professor of fine art and English literature at William Carey University and Mississippi Gulf Coast Community College on the MS Gulf Coast. She is a freelance writer for *The Sun Herald* and *See South Mississippi*. Cummings also has a passion for creative writing and has many poems, plays, and books in the works.

Cummings loves travel, theater, opera, art museums, coffee shops and ballroom dancing. She has an obsession for vintage fashion and frequently blogs about her quest for cloche hats and swing dresses. Her greatest artistic influences have been Oscar Wilde, the Romantic poets, The Pre-Raphaelites and Gustav Klimt.

Residing in Gautier, MS, since 1998, **Judy Davies** writes poetry and prose and manages the music publishing company for her composer husband, Ken Davies. They released their first CD of narrated poetry with custom crafted music, *Poetic Soundscapes,* in 2012. Judy's book, *Poetic Images,* was released in 2011. Published in the U.S. and abroad, she is vice-president of the Mississippi Poetry Society, an active South Branch member, and the 2012 Senior

Poet Laureate for Mississippi. Judy holds degrees in English and Paralegal Studies. She and Ken are frequent travelers to both music and poetry festivals. For further information: www.kendavies.net/judyswriting.

Brenda Brown Finnegan joined the Round Island Lighthouse Preservation Society in 1998, shortly before Hurricane Georges toppled it, and worked diligently on behalf of the lighthouse until Katrina, in 2005, washed away her home on Belle Fontaine Beach. She was working on a history of the lighthouse, but all of her records, including reference materials and photos were lost in the storm.

A graduate of the University of Southern Mississippi, she belongs to the Mississippi Poetry Society and Gulf Coast Writers Association. She and her husband, Deacon Martin Finnegan, reared their three children in Pascagoula, where they lived for 25 years before moving to the Ocean Springs area.

Keith Goodfellow is a physician and freelance outdoor writer. He lives in Gulfport, Mississippi with his wife and four children. Earning a B.S. from Tulane University and an M.S. from the University of New Orleans, his main area study was ichthyology. He received a doctorate of medicine degree from L.S.U. School of Medicine in New Orleans. Having fished the northern Gulf of Mexico for five decades, he has been published in several regional outdoor magazines, as well as, scientific journals, and the Louisiana English Journal.

Stanley Hastings, a native of Port Gibson, Mississippi, is a retired school and public librarian, still working as a church organist and freelance writer. He holds degrees from Hinds Community College and the University of Southern Mississippi, and has lived in Gulfport, Mississippi, since 1977.

W. Michiel Hawkins grew up at Moore Tower on the Bienville National Forest near Forest, Mississippi. Living in the National Forest provided an education filled with animals, birds, trees and plants. Each day and each season was filled with changes observed and recorded. From this viewpoint Michiel Hawkins continues to share this knowledge in poetry, short stories and creative nonfiction.

Author **Marilyn Johnston** lives in historic Mobile, Alabama. She is the author of the suspense/romance novel *Deadly Star* written under the pen name of "cj petterson" and published in 2013 by Crimson Romance. Her fiction and non-fiction short stories have appeared in several anthologies.

A veteran of communication media in the corporate world, Marilyn began writing for pleasure after she retired from the auto industry. She is a member of Sisters in Crime, the Society for Children's Book Writers and Illustrators, and a charter member of the Mobile Writers Guild.

Visit cj petterson on her shared blog at www.lyricalpens.com.

Karen B. Kurtz began collecting antique dolls when she was 12. Today, she is a doll historian, author, and lecturer. A former schoolteacher, journalist, editor, college administrator, publisher, and consultant, Kurtz received a prestigious grant from United Federation of Doll Clubs (Kansas City) to document Civil War dolls, circa 1830-1870. Providence led her to Bellingrath Gardens and Home, where she discovered china doll heads dating near the period of her research project. She has published two books with Pearson and more than 500 articles for adults and children. Kurtz divides her time between the Eastern Shore of Mobile Bay and Northern Indiana.

Sherryl LaPointe began writing as a child when she often wrote plays for production by Sherryl and her sisters. She used her writing throughout her career as an elementary school teacher, largely for use in her own classroom. More recently, she has written for local publications. In addition to teaching, Sherryl served with her husband and daughter as children's evangelists, traveling to various churches in the South. During this period, she wrote the materials for use with the children. Sherryl lives in Gulfport, Mississippi with her husband and enjoys the frequent company of her daughter who lives in the vicinity.

Philip L Levin MD serves as president of the 160-member Gulf Coast Writers Association, based on the Mississippi Coast, as well as editor of its publications, such as this anthology and their magazine, *The Magnolia Quarterly.* Among his published works are dozens of articles for local and national magazines, award winning stories and poems, and over a dozen books, including the award winning children's book, *"Ndovu the Elephant."* Professionally, he's worked thirty-five years as an emergency medicine physician and travels regularly to foreign countries where he volunteers his medical abilities in rural hospitals, clinics, and leper colonies.

To date, **Valerie Livengood** has spent her entire life living in coastal states, moving from the Pacific to the Atlantic and ending up on the Gulf Coast. Much of the last 20+ years has been engaged with homeschooling her five children. She served as academic coordinator on the board of a homeschool support group with over 200 families and published the group's newsletter for several years. With her kids now grown, she has turned to writing, as well as continuing to volunteer with local Friends of the Library and HOPE Adult Learning, an adult literacy ministry.

Elaine McDermott is the author of essays and articles, including *"Poetry Across the Curriculum"* for the National Institute for Staff and Organizational Development, the University of Texas at Austin. However, her main obsession is writing poetry. In 1995, she received a grant sponsored by the Mississippi Humanities Council for her presentation of her poems, *"Poetry: Understanding the Human Condition."* She received a Bachelor's Degree in English from University of Southern Mississippi and a Master's Degree from William Carey University. She has authored several collections of poetry. Many of her poems are centered around her native New Orleans and the Mississippi Gulf Coast. Elaine retired as Learning Lab Director from MGCCC, Jefferson Davis Campus.

Fowler McLain is the pen name for the writing team of Norman Fowler and Kathryn McLain. After years of writing separately, Norman and Kathryn joined forces in 2006 and have one contemporary crime novel on the shelf, a southern caper waiting a verdict from two publishers, and a third in progress.

Sue Townley Monkress, an Oklahoma native transplanted to the South six years ago, has immersed herself in the beauty and culture of the Gulf Coast. She is a former Marketing and Tax Analyst for a major oil company. Three of her books are published by Lulu.com and her articles and short stories have been included in various anthologies and magazines.

Jamie Jones O'Quinn is a freelance writer, photographer, and former editor. This University of Southern Mississippi and Mississippi College graduate works at The Children's Center at Southern Miss.

She has over 250 published magazine and newspaper articles, co-authored Forrest General Hospital's book *"Forrest The Little Deer"*, was contributing writer and photographer for Hattiesburg's 125th Anniversary Celebration book, founded a syndicated column, and the Hattiesburg Chapter of the Mississippi Writers Guild.

She enjoys flicking sawdust out of her hair while watching the world champion chainsaw artist carve, laughing at tall tales with the guitar maker in his workshop, and dancing with the Choctaw Indians.

Deanna Vogt is a happy transplant to the Mississippi Gulf Coast. She is an executive coach and researcher with a special interest in ordinary genius, and the sparks and work styles that lead to creative work, innovation, invention and discovery. She writes about these topics at DeannaVogt.com.